PROSPERING IN A PANDEMIC!

"CREATE WEALTH WITH YOUR HEALTH"
BLOOD MONEY!

PROSPERING IN A PANDEMIC!

"CREATE WEALTH WITH YOUR HEALTH"

MAKE THOUSAND$ MONTHLY...
NO MONEY OR SKILL NEEDED!!!
DUMMIES GUIDE TO CLINICAL TRIALS
"BLOOD MONEY"

gatekeeper press
Columbus, Ohio

The views and opinions expressed in this book are solely those of the author and do not reflect the views or opinions of Gatekeeper Press. Gatekeeper Press is not to be held responsible for and expressly disclaims responsibility of the content herein.

Prospering in a Pandemic! "Create Wealth with Your Health": "Make Thousands Monthly...No Money or Skill Needed!!! DUMMIES GUIDE TO CLINICAL TRIALS "BLOOD MONEY!"

Published by Gatekeeper Press

2167 Stringtown Rd., Suite 109

Columbus, OH 43123-2989

www.GatekeeperPress.com

Copyright © 2022 by G King

All rights reserved. Neither this book, nor any parts within it may be sold or reproduced in any form or by any electronic or mechanical means, including information storage and retrieval systems, without permission in writing from the author. The only exception is by a reviewer, who may quote short excerpts in a review.

Library of Congress Control Number: 2020944906

ISBN (paperback): 9781662904240

eISBN: 9781662904257

CONTENTS

INTRODUCTION	1
SCREENING	35
CHECK-IN	45
THE STUDY	51
LESS RISK/STAY HEALTHY	57
LIST OF CLINICAL FACILITIES	81
ABOUT THE AUTHOR	89
CONCLUSION	93

INTRODUCTION

First, I would like to thank everyone for their purchase of *Prospering in a Pandemic*. I'm sure that most of you will be thanking me later, when you find yourself in a better financial position after reading and applying the simple instructions I provided for you in this guide. And as they always say, the best form of thanking is a referral or good reviews & ratings!

    I would like to add that this is not a get-rich-quick scheme, nor will you make millions of dollars doing it. However, if you're in decent health and apply the information that I provided for you, there is no reason why you can't have a few extra thousand dollars in your pocket in a single month or so. I often hear of potential small business ventures who are in need of seed money to start a business but can't come up with the capital, or a person who needs a 3% down payment on a house, etc. Well, in comes *Prospering in a Pandemic*, because I honestly can not think of a better way for a person with little or no skill to raise money than this.

    This is not your traditional book. I will not make this long and drawn out like many publications do. I will only concentrate on topics and specifics that I think are imperative for one to successfully make money in this field.

Welcome to the world of medical studies, clinical trials, and studies, aka lab rats. Please do not get discouraged by the titles. Because, besides doing a great deal of good for humanity, I know quite a few people who have made a decent living from this and were able to purchase new vehicles as well as homes. In addition, I know many who have used their proceeds to travel domestically and internationally.

I'm pretty sure when most people think of medical studies, they get a picture in their head of someone lying on an operating table with tubes in their body and blood and guts everywhere... lol. This cannot be further from the truth! The fact of the matter is that it is usually the complete opposite, which is a calm and relaxed atmosphere in which you are amongst an average of about 10 (more or less) people who are being tested as well. In a nutshell, you are being given a lower-mg dose pill or injection (possibly escalating higher) so researchers can see the effects as well as the metabolism of the drug. Most pharmaceutical companies usually start off giving much higher doses to animals to see how well they tolerate it before giving that drug to humans at much lower doses. Outside of the PK (Pharmacokinetic) day, which is the heavy-testing and multiple blood draw day, most of the other days you're basically hanging out, eating, on the computer/phone, or doing other things to occupy your downtime, which you have a lot of. I will get more into that in a later chapter.

But before I go any further, I would like to very quickly disprove the myth of medical studies, or better yet, prove how they are no more unsafe than most of the activities we do and food we eat every day. I believe most of us are already lab rats, experimenting with the foods that we eat daily. The majority of the foods we eat today are GMO (genetically modified organisms), which are not good for the human body. If they were, then why would companies brag about their one or two products that aren't a GMO and post it all over the package label trying to convince the public that it's a healthier choice? A lot of fast foods aren't even real food, more like Frankenfood. It is difficult, and expensive, to purchase good/fresh food today because the majority of it is tainted with hazardous ingredients. Even a lot of vegetables are loaded with pesticides or are crossbred/hybrid.

I will list a few things below that will give a more clear and conclusive picture to support my theory on why medical studies are no worse than our everyday consumption of food/air/water.

Every single day of our lives, we, as humans, ingest harmful, dangerous, and often deadly toxins. Whether it's through our food, the air, our phones, lotions, drinks, etc., toxins are entering our body, and the worst part is, this is more than likely a daily occurrence, which over time will take its toll on the body, leading to many harmful illnesses.

The ultimate goal for most food companies is profit, and in order to achieve this, they need their product to have a long shelf life (expiration date). They want their products to be able to remain on the shelf for months/years (mostly canned goods, but this applies to most foods), making the chances greater of selling before the expiration date arrives. That's why just about all of today's foods are loaded heavily with salt/sodium, etc. as preservatives, to keep them edible for a long time. But these preservatives cause many health problems, including high blood pressure and heart problems.

The FDA allows many things in our foods that the majority of the public probably has no idea of and many would be disgusted by if they did. Here is a list of just a few of the things that can be found in the US food supply, which is approved by the US Food and Drug Administration:

1) Insect Filth (urine/feces)
2) Rodent Filth (hair, etc.)
3) Mold
4) Insects (physical)
5) Mammalian Excreta (aka rat poop)
6) Rot
7) Larvae
8) Insect Eggs
9) Parasites
10) Mildew
11) Sand and Grit
12) Foreign Matter
13) Banned GMO Chinese rice
14) Maggot or fly eggs

15) Cigarette butts or sticks

And what's even worse about this is, from what I have been told by someone who works in this field, FDA inspections only happen at manufacturing facilities on average about every two to three years. If it does miraculously happen annually, it would be a huge anomaly! And if/when it happens it is very casual, putting most of the responsibility on the manufacturers themselves for the overall food safety and quality, which is a very scary thought!

Scientists finally issued a warning against canola oil, admitting that it damages your brain and can cause dementia and weight gain! The biggest risk of consuming foods that contain canola oil are as follows:

- depletes vitamin E from the body
- leaves no foul taste or smell when it's spoiled, making it hard to tell if you're eating rancid erucic acid
- opens the door for free radicals, undermining natural antioxidants, and is linked to increased incidents of many diseases
- molds quickly and inhibits enzyme function
- daily consumption can raise your triglycerides over 40%
- can shorten the lifespan of animals and lower platelet count
- may cause an increase of lung cancers in humans
- Because of high sulfur content, it goes rancid easily, which can aggravate allergies and compound problems for people with asthmatic or bronchial issues.

- And lastly, it increases the rigidity of membranes, which can trigger degenerative diseases.

Just recently in Ireland, an Irish court ruled that Subway bread is not real bread!

If you eat fried foods, you make it almost impossible for your digestive system to nourish your body properly because the overheated fat interferes with the function of the liver. Fried foods are also high in fat, calories, and salt, making it a high risk for obesity, high blood pressure, and high cholesterol. Recent studies have even linked it to death.

Next is simple tap water. A plethora of studies have tested the water supplies in many US cities/towns, and the same indisputable conclusions have been made. A very large amount of the US water supply is contaminated with all types of poison. As many as 63 million people – nearly 1/5 of the US from California to NYC – are exposed to potentially unsafe water. The EPA estimates local water systems will need to invest up to $384 billion in the coming decades to keep our drinking/plumbing water clean. Some of the toxins found in your tap water include chlorine, chloride, lead, iron, arsenic, copper, and hydrogen sulfide. In addition, it may also contain other undesirable contaminants like toxic metal salts, pesticides, and, most disturbing to me, growth hormones, including estrogen!

But at the top of most professionals' list of tap water dangers is PFQA/PFOS (perfluorooctanoic acid), also part of a class compound called PFAS (perfluoroalkyl and polyfluoroalkyl substances). Studies have shown certain PFAS compounds may affect the growth, learning, and behavior of infants and children, lower a woman's chances of getting pregnant, interfere with the body's natural hormones, increase cholesterol levels, affect the immune system, and increase cancer risks. Laboratory animals exposed to high doses of one or more PFAS compounds showed changes in liver, thyroid, and pancreatic function. And these are just a few of the dangers of US drinking water.

And you're not 100% safe with bottled water because most of those are not much better than your tap/home water when it comes to fluoride and electrolytes. Many contain fluoride, while most others don't have electrolytes in them, which help the body tremendously because it contains certain minerals that carry electrical charges responsible for stimulating healthy muscles and nerves.

Tilapia, the fourth most-consumed seafood in America, has facts about it that most people probably don't know. Because it is not available in the wild, there are concerns that tilapia is no longer a real fish but a "frankenfish"! Now here comes the worst part— the majority of these farms feed the fish GMO corn, algae, and soy, which breeds toxic protein harmful to humans. Here are five reasons you should stay away from tilapia:

1. Recent studies have found that farm-raised tilapia may cause inflammation.
2. Farmed fish may have at least 10x the amount of cancer-causing organic pollutants compared to the wild variety.

3. Farm-bred fish have been found to have high concentrations of antibiotics and pesticides.
4. Farm-bred fish have lower levels of healthy nutrients.
5. Dioxin levels are 11x higher in farm-bred fish compared to wild fish.

Everyone wants to look youthful these days, and vanity is at an all-time high! One of the main focuses is our hair. By our mid-thirties, it's either falling out or turning grey. We know you can go the wig, weave, plug, etc. route if it falls out, but for the greying part, most turn to hair dyes. Here is a little secret that most people don't know about hair dyes. Many of them contain ingredients that increase the risk of cancer and brain tumors! The FDA also reports eye injuries, including blindness, from permanent hair dyes. Toxic chemicals used in many hair dyes include:

- p-Phenylenediamine - linked to skin sensitization and cancer
- Resorcinol - linked to organ system toxicity and hormone disruption
- Lead acetate - linked to neurotoxicity
- Toluene - linked to liver/kidney damage, birth defects, and pregnancy loss

Aspartame, the artificial sweetener and sugar substitute contained in some foods and beverages that millions of Americans consume daily, is considered by some to be one of the most dangerous substances on the market today. Aspartame has been linked to a multitude of ailments, including:

- cancer
- seizures
- headaches
- depression
- attention deficit disorder
- dizziness
- weight gain
- birth defects

White sugar is a refined carbohydrate and is technically classified as a drug/neurotoxin. It would take four pancreases to process white sugar; the human body only has one. White sugar stresses the pancreas, kidney, and liver; starves the brain of oxygen; causes adrenal weakness, baldness, attention deficits, blindness, tooth decay, high blood pressure, allergies, bone loss, infertility, glaucoma, nerve damage (i.e. Multiple Sclerosis), brain damage (Alzheimer's), senility, kidney failure, diabetes, mood swings, hyperactivity, and arthritis, amongst many more ailments. White sugar also feeds cancer cells and stimulates tumor growth. A study was done that hooked rats on cocaine and sugar. When given a choice between both, the rats overwhelmingly picked the sugar!

Something as simple as a tooth-filling can have health hazards. I say this because most fillings are silver amalgam fillings. These particular fillings contain mercury, which can be toxic because this metal can seep into the bloodstream, causing many health issues.

Even cosmetics as simple as everyday lotions and creams can cause cancer. It has been scientifically proven that when some of these cosmetics come in direct contact with the skin, it can increase the chances of getting prostate or ovarian cancer.

If you read the back of, let's say, a grape soda can, you will not find grapes anywhere on the list of ingredients. It's artificially flavored, but it smells and tastes like grapes. This is due to the chemicals added. The chemical capital of the US is in New Jersey, and they're so good at what they do, they can probably make cow manure taste like a juicy hamburger.

Speaking of soda, it has been linked to obesity, depression, cancer, and cardiovascular disease, among a whole lot of other ailments. Added sugar can have disastrous effects on your health. However, some sources of sugar are worse than others, and sugary *drinks* are the worst, by far!

An experienced butcher recently admitted that when he, as well as the majority of other butchers, would see "obvious" cancers in the pork that he was cutting, he would just cut around the discolored meat, discard that small portion, and sell the remainder of it to customers.

Many french fries and potato chip brands contain enormous amounts of fat and sodium. Many of them also contain acrylamide, a chemical that adds an increased risk of infertility and several forms of cancer.

Recently, 45 fruit juices were tested and found to contain at least one heavy metal, inorganic arsenic, mercury, lead, arsenic, and/or cadmium, a soft, silvery-white metal that is dangerous in high levels. Breathing it can lead to death. Being exposed at lower levels over a long period of time can cause damage to the kidneys, lungs, and bones. Metals found in at least seven of the samples taken have the most potential harm to children who drink at least half a cup per day. Overall, the risk of long-term exposure to heavy metals can damage the ability to learn, as well as cause kidney disease, high blood pressure, diabetes, and certain types of cancer.

This one might be a surprise to everyone, especially males. Nonstick frying pans can lead to smaller penis size, study says. A new study found that a chemical commonly found on nonstick pans and fast-food wrappers may have a significant impact on the male penis size. Males who have been exposed to PFCs (perfluorochemicals) had significantly smaller penis sizes as well as lower semen count/quality. PFCs are chemicals commonly used as water and oil repellents in cookware and textiles.

Did you know that public hand dryers suck in fecal bacteria and often blow it back onto your hands?! Recent studies have shown that fecal bacteria shoot into the air when an open toilet seat is flushed. It's a new phenomenon that is grossly known as "toilet plume." That's right, when a toilet is flushed, little bits of poop and bacteria can be thrown as high as 15 ft into the air and often finds itself landing in the hand dryers, which turns around and blows it right back onto the hands of the person attempting to dry them.

Apples have a very low resistance to pests, so they have to be heavily sprayed with pesticide spray, which is harmful to the human body. Whenever possible, buy organic! And speaking of apples (I'm using apples as a proxy for most fruits), it has been estimated that it would take 20 apples today to have the same nutrients as an apple from, let's say, the pre-1930s.

Even something as simple as plastic, thermos, and now aluminum water bottles (and plates) can be toxic. Studies have shown that drinking beverages, including water, from plastic bottles increases the risk of cancer, especially if the temperature is warm/hot or it has been microwaved, thus slightly melting the plastic, allowing the toxin bisphenol A (BPA) to seep into your food or beverage.

Ramen Noodles have been linked to chronic inflammation, weight gain, Alzheimer's, and Parkinson's disease, mainly because the noodles don't break down after digestion. These are very frequently purchased and eaten by college students and prison inmates.

Earlier this year, a Canadian investigative consumer program ordered DNA analysis of several fast-food chicken sandwiches. The test concluded that Subway chicken was only half meat, the other half was soy. I'm sure a lot of people will say that's not a bad thing. Well, think again!

Soy foods are high in phytoestrogens, which are plant-based substances that mimic the effects of estrogen in the body by altering hormone levels and potentially reducing testosterone, which, of course, reduces a male's ability to have satisfying sex as well as his sex drive and performance. Even worse, high levels of estrogen have been linked to an increased risk of breast cancer.

Toothpaste, as well as simple water, contains fluoride. I know what you have been taught, but fluoride is not good for the body. Look at the back of your toothpaste and read the drug facts. It clearly lists the drug "sodium fluoride" and also says "Do not swallow, if so contact the Poison Control Center immediately." The amount they are talking about is a pea-sized ¼ milligram, the same amount in the average size eight-ounce glass of tap water.

Most developed countries around the world and most of Europe do not consume fluoridated water and some even ban the use of it. The countries that have banned fluoride have not seen any increase in tooth decay, cavities, etc. This is why the FDA requires a poison warning on every tube of fluoride toothpaste now sold in the US. Risk from ingesting fluoride toothpaste includes permanent tooth discoloration, stomach ailments, acute toxicity, skin rashes, and impairment in glucose metabolism. Worse still, Harvard researchers have linked fluoride to ADHD, Autism, and other childhood mental health disorders. I personally buy only non-fluoride toothpaste.

FYI – on the bottom of every tube of toothpaste is a colored label (square). Each color represents a specific ingredient. Green = Natural, Blue = Natural + Medicine, Red = Natural + Chemical, and Black = Pure Chemical.

Did you know that the four and five digit PLU (price look-up) code on some foods stands for something? When it starts with a three or four and has four digits, it's "conventionally grown." When it starts with nine and has five digits, it's "organically grown." When it starts with eight and has five digits, it's "genetically modified."

Reported in August 2019: UK teen goes blind after only eating fried food, chips, and white bread since elementary school.

Talcum or baby powder, which millions of people use on a daily basis, can be toxic. Many people use it for hygienic purposes, often on the genital area. This can be very harmful to females because this powder contains a substance known as asbestos, which may be responsible for ovarian cancer. When in direct contact with the vagina, it can seep through and enter a female's ovaries. In 2016, a St. Louis jury awarded a California woman more than $70 million in her lawsuit against Johnson & Johnson alleging using their baby powder for years caused her cancer.

Below is a list of a few diseases and illnesses, other than mesothelioma and ovarian cancer, linked to talcum powder use:

- breast cancer
- diabetes
- kidney stones
- heart disease
- osteoporosis
- multiple sclerosis
- strokes
- rheumatoid arthritis

Vitamin-fortified milk began to appear in the 1920s and was common by the 1930s. When we hear the slogan "Drink your milk to get your daily nutrition of vitamin D" one would assume that the milk naturally has vitamin D in it. It doesn't! Vitamin D is added to the milk. Which basically means that they can add it to any liquid such as soda, alcoholic beverages, etc., and tell the public to drink that to get your daily dose of vitamin D.

Cheese is another dairy product that is terrible for the human body. I will list a few alarming facts about cheese and your health to further prove this statement:

- Cheese has become American's #1 source of saturated fat. No wonder the US has an obesity epidemic!
- Many kinds of cheese are made using an animal's stomach enzyme, mainly from rennet that comes from calves' stomach linings.
- Cheese can contain pus from a cow's bladder infection, making cheese an unhealthy food choice due to poor manufacturing practices.
- The cows are treated like milk-producing machines and are genetically pumped full of antibiotics and hormones to produce more milk. Cows suffer through this process, and humans who drink their milk increase their chances of developing heart disease, diabetes, cancer, and many other ailments.
- Eating cheese can cause diabetes and heart disease.
- Cheesemakers spray on mold to make the rind, the outside layer that forms on cheese during the cheese-making and aging process. Yes, that's correct. Cheese can contain mold content.
- There are plenty of videos on YouTube of people trying to burn processed cheese using a cigarette lighter. The results are: the cheese doesn't melt how you think it should melt; instead, it's burning like plastic with black smoke coming off of it.

- Dairy has also been linked to weaker bones and osteoporosis. A study found that the more dairy a person consumes, the higher his or her risk of osteoporosis and hip fractures.

I'm going to list a few things about margarine that you probably don't know.

- Margarine was originally developed as an animal feed because it was a cheap and tasty substitute for butter that would store easily on ships.
- Margarine is one molecule away from being plastic. Yes – plastic!
- Margarine is high in trans-fatty acids and increases cardiovascular disease risk.
- Margarine doesn't decompose at room temperature, like butter, proving margarine has no nutritional value.

Cigarettes – we've all heard the dangers of smoking cigarettes, but the ones who continue to smoke don't care enough to stop. To support this, I will give a few facts about the dangers of smoking. Cigarette smoking harms nearly *every* organ in the body, causes many diseases, and reduces the health of smokers in general. Along with:

- Cardiovascular disease
- Respiratory disease

- Cancer almost anywhere in the body
    - Bladder
    - Blood
    - Cervix
    - Colon and rectum
    - Esophagus
    - Kidney and ureter
    - Larynx
    - Liver
    - Pancreas
    - Stomach
    - Trachea, bronchus, and lungs
    - Oropharynx (throat, tongue, soft palate, and tonsils)

Marijuana – also known as cannabis or weed – is the most commonly used of all illicit drugs and is slowly becoming legal in many US states. Marijuana has always been looked at as non-lethal, doing no bodily harm to its users. This might have been somewhat correct decades ago, but I can assure you that this is far, far from correct. Marijuana from, let's say, the 1980s, or back when Bob Marley was smoking it, might have actually been doing a little good for the smoker. But weed today is not the same, and most is filled with additives that are not healthy. Just to name a few, some of the ingredients, such as medroxyprogesterone acetate (Depo-Provera), block the development of masculinity and promote femininity by reducing testosterone and boosting estrogen.

The short-term effects of marijuana include:

- Distorted perception (sights, sounds, touch)
- Problems with memory and learning
- Loss of coordination
- Trouble thinking and problem-solving
- Increased heart rate and reduced blood pressure

It also affects your brain, your heart, your bones, and your lungs. But most of all, studies have linked marijuana smoking to lung cancer. The fact that marijuana smoke contains three times the amount of tar found in tobacco smoke and 50 percent more carcinogens, it would seem logical that this is correct.

While we're on the subject of recreational smoking, let's not leave out hookah. Hookah has become the most popular flavored tobacco product among young adults. But many dangers come with smoking hookah because it has many of the same health risks of smoking cigarettes. The charcoal used to heat the tobacco can raise health risks by producing high levels of carbon monoxide, metals, and cancer-causing chemicals. I know some smokers think it's safe because of the H_2O but even after it has passed through the water, the smoke from a hookah still has high levels of toxic agents.

The first ever hookah smoking-related death was reported in the summer of 2019. And here's a quick fact about hookah that most people might not know. The average hookah session is about one hour which amounts to about 200 puffs. In that amount of time a smoker would consume the equivalent of about 100 cigarettes from just one of these sessions.

Microwave ovens make your food radioactive and can release harmful radiation, which raises your risk of cancer as well as cataracts. They're known to destroy the health and nutrients in your food, which increases your risk of nutrient deficiencies in the body. Microwaves also cause plastic containers to release harmful chemicals into your already affected food.

CTE (Chronic Traumatic Encephalopathy) is being diagnosed in many football and boxing athletes. In short, it's a progressive degenerative/neurodegenerative disease of the brain, which causes loss of memory and confusion as well as flawed judgment. It can also cause changes in one's mood, personality, and behavior, which can include depression, anxiety, and suicidal thoughts and actions, as well as aggression. But yet, even with all of this knowledge, thousands of athletes still wish to play and many wish to pursue a boxing and/or football career. Hundreds of millions of viewers and fans still support this, knowing the effects it has on the athlete's body.

Let's face it, almost every prescription/OTC drug on the market has a few side effects. And people still take these drugs daily! If you listen to any commercial advertising these products, you will always hear at the end a very quick rundown of side effects or ailments that can happen to a percentage of the population who take that particular drug. The key word is "daily." Daily usage over time has a greater risk of some of those ailments to occur. But when you take any of these same drugs during a clinical trial, you will more than likely only take this medication one single time or maybe daily for a week or two, drastically reducing the chances of permanent or long-lasting damage.

Also, almost half of adult Americans are medicated, which means that almost one out of two people in the US (46% of the population) used one or more prescription/OTC drugs in a 12-month period. And every last one of these drugs has been through the clinical testing pipelines.

As far as foods go, there's an old saying: Don't go to the supermarket when you're starving! Meaning, try as much as possible not to entice yourself with food that you know is not good for you.

There are over forty different studies with overwhelming evidence that confirm GMO foods (the majority of US supermarket foods) are destroying our health. The additives to most foods today are so addictive that most people would rather choose slow suffering, or even death, versus changing their diet.

And let's be honest with ourselves, even after reading this the average person is not going to stop eating/doing the things I mentioned above. So like I've been saying, you might as well get paid to do a medical study because the money is good and you're already being exposed to worse. So please, all the food and water companies, etc. don't get upset due to the information in this book because trust me you won't lose many customers over it.Most people are way too hooked to change their habits!

Like I previously alluded to, every single medication, prescription, and over-the-counter drug currently on the market has gone through the clinical trial pipeline. Most start off being tested on animals such as rats, monkeys, dogs, etc. Usually the amount given to animals is at a much higher dosage than what's given to humans. Something else to consider is the fact that plenty of drug companies are retesting plenty of medications that are already on the market for a multitude of reasons. So basically it's like purchasing a bottle of, let's say, Tylenol from a store, taking a few of them for a couple of days, giving some blood and getting paid a few thousand dollars. That is no exaggeration in some clinical trial cases.

Another important thing I would like to mention is that every single time you are interested in a study, you have to "screen" for that study. This means that you have to take a blood test that measures your blood levels and have vitals (blood pressure), EKGs, BMI, etc. checked before you can be deemed healthy enough to participate in that particular study. I emphasize this because if you just did a previous study and your labs are good enough to do another study, then there's a great chance that you're still in great health and weren't affected by the study that you just did or any of the other ones you might have done in the past. And I personally know people who have been doing clinical trials for a few years, and some even over a decade, that can still easily pass these screenings.

I would also like to mention that you will get educated on your body and learn many things about your personal health that you would never have known if you didn't do medical studies. Most subjects who have been in the study game for a few years become knowledgeable on the human body learning good vital sign numbers, EKG readings, etc. As for me personally, I found out that I had a small brain aneurysm after getting a head scan for a study. This is something that I probably would never have found out. Most people die without ever knowing they had an aneurysm because it can live dormant in the body for decades without you ever knowing it. So you find out about your complete health, which is a very big plus. And the best part about it is that it's free. If you had to pay out of pocket, this bill can go into the thousands.

One of the main allies a study subject has in their corner is the IRB. The IRB (Institutional Review Board) is an ethics committee of both scientists and non-scientists who review, modify, approve or disapprove research studies by following federal laws and guidelines. This organization is also required by federal regulations to provide periodic review of ongoing research studies. Anytime during or after participation in a research study a subject can contact them with any questions or concerns, which can also be done anonymously.

And lastly, I'm very aware that in the US there have been some very unethical medical experiments that have been performed on unknowing subjects (Tuskegee Experiment, etc). But what makes this different is one major thing and that is something called, "informed consent." Everything from the biggest to the smallest thing that is going to be performed, could happen or presumed can happen to you, will be listed in this consent. By law, they have to FULLY explain (in your language) the entire rundown of all the risks and dangers that could possibly affect you during that particular study that you are screening for. It is your decision whether or not you feel comfortable enough to continue.

Those are just a few examples to prove my theory that the average person is already a lab rat. Eating and doing everyday activities are just as or more harmful than doing an average medical study. I can write a full book (I'm sure plenty already exist) further proving this, but if you don't agree with me after all of this evidence then you never will.

So in a nutshell, this book will educate the public on the whole process and also teach anyone interested in making money in this field how to successfully go about this process. Everything from how to initially start the process, where to go, who to call, and how to go about it in the safest manner.

If an experimental drug is deemed safely tolerated by animals, the next step is for humans to start the testing process. The process is divided into phases:

- **Phase I**: Researchers test a treatment or new drug with a small group of people for the first time to evaluate its safety, identify side effects and how it breaks down in the bloodstream, and determine a safe dosage range.
- **Phase II**: The drug or treatment is given to a larger group of people to see if it is effective and to further evaluate its safety. Both generic and brand names are used and tested to compare differences and similarities.

- **Phase III:** The treatment or drug is given to a large group of people to confirm its effectiveness, monitor side effects, compare it to commonly used treatments, and collect information that will allow the treatment or drug to be used safely.
- **Phase IV:** Studies are done after the treatment or drug has been marketed to gather information on the drug's effect in various populations and any side effects associated with long-term use.

Some of this gets really technical and hard to understand, but here's the bottom line to all of this. In all my years of being a tech, and participating in clinical trials, I can personally assure you that getting ill to the point of needing hospital or emergency room treatment is very rare. The most common thing I've witnessed was headaches, stomachaches, rashes (and those are infrequent), and maybe someone feeling a little woozy or just not completely themselves temporarily.

Now I'm not saying there have't been people who needed medical attention or a particular study that had to be stopped after being deemed unsafe, but if it did it would be somewhat of an anomaly. When and if it does happen, patients are very well taken care of because a lot of testing facilities are inside hospitals or are in very close proximity to one. Also, on-staff are always RN's or MD's who are more than prepared for such an event. Word of any incident makes its way throughout most of the other pharmaceutical communities very quickly and most participants usually know exactly where and (most importantly) what medication was being used, which makes most scratch that one off their list of studies not to do.

Picking and choosing which study you might want to do as well as might not want to do is very important in one's career as a clinical trial subject. I will dive further into this subject in a later chapter.

I know the biggest thing people want to know is, how much do medical studies pay? Well, that question doesn't have a quick or simple answer because the range of payment is so wide. The amount of days the study is going to be, the facility itself, what the study consists of, etc., will all determine how much a particular study will pay out.

Well, for the price of this book, you can make your money back just from screening (doing bloodwork, consenting, etc.) at some facilities. For instance, Parexel in Baltimore pays $20 cash just to screen. Pfizer in Connecticut pays $135 for every screening, plus if you have a second test, usually that same day, you get an additional $135, so you can make up to $270 for an estimated five to seven hour screening. Clini-Labs in NYC pays anywhere between $125 to $200 just to screen. There was a location in Philadelphia (no longer open for testing) that paid each participant who screened $50 plus their traveling fees. So what a few subjects would do is buy a first-class, round-trip Amtrak ticket from, let's say, NYC to Philadelphia, which at that time was around $370. They would never get on the train but would then drive or take the bus down instead and get a refund on the Amtrak ticket and would make a little over $400 just to screen for a single study! Covance Clinical Trials had studies where they would pay you $250 just to screen and another $250 if you check-in, on the condition that your address is over 100 miles away. So that would be an extra $500 on top of the total study compensation you can make. Also, some facilities are currently paying from $50 to $100 for every Covid test you take.

There are small outpatient studies that do not require any overnight stays. They usually pay anywhere from $50 to a few hundred dollars. But if you're doing an inpatient study (overnight stays) which the majority of subjects want, I always tell people that $300 a night is the standard. If you make more than that (which is very, very common) you are ahead of the game. If you are making less than that, you might need to look more closely into if you want to do that particular study. Example: if you do a 20-day inpatient study, then your total pay should be somewhere around $6,000 (20 days x $300 a day). I'm not saying that I would tell someone not to do a study under $300 a day, I'm just saying that you should evaluate what exactly is involved in that particular one. It might be really easy and, even more important, local, making it well worth the money. I'm just saying to do your due diligence.

I have seen payouts smaller and I have seen payouts a lot higher. I have been in one that paid $4,290 for only thirteen days ($330 a day). I've seen twenty-five days for $9,200 ($368 a day). I have seen $12,000 total payout studies. The most I have ever seen for a non-NASA study was a little over $29,000 for six months (in and out). I did a six-day study for $3,450 ($575 a day) and a study that paid $2,400 for four days - that's $600 a day! A friend of mine just did a four-day for $3,500. But on the flip side, I have seen some that only paid $5,000 for twenty-five days ($200 a day) and six days for $1,100 ($183 a day). Parexel in California had studies that paid around $7,000 for only twenty days - that's $350 per day. So as you can see, the pay per-day and full total payout can vary, but if I had to estimate I would say that the average inpatient study is around $3,500 in total payout at an average of $300 a day.

Also, there are the infamous NASA studies that have been around for decades. The pay on this fluctuates depending on the particular study. But I will give info on one of their main studies. There's one that lasts for about two months that pays $19,000 in which you will be paid weekly while you're there to pay your bills, etc. The first two weeks are to prepare you for all that you would have to endure, including strenuous training and familarization. The last two weeks are for rehabilitation and getting your body back to normal. And the weeks in between involve laying in bed for over a month, simulating a weightless astronaut in space in which you would have to eat, wash your clothes, shower, use the toilet, etc., all while laying down, at all times!

Below, I list very recent (2021) study listings and payouts from one specific research clinic who still contacts me whenever a study becomes available:

Amount	Days	O/P visits	
$2,700.00	8	1	
$6,000.00	17	1	
$3,000.00	5	0	($50 screen)
$4,100.00	14	1	

Prospering in a Pandemic

Amount	Days	O/P visits
$1,500.00	3	1
$4,150.00	11	1
$3,600.00	10	1
$4,000.00	14	1
$5,050.00	18	1
$3,600.00	10	1
$2,050.00	6	1
$10,650.00	32 (8 days x 4)	2
$3,000.00	10	1
$4,453.00	17	1
$7,200.00	24	2
$5,100.00	19	1
$6,800.00	26	1
$8,720.00	31	1
$13,000.00	44	0
$14,000.00	36 (9 days x 4)	0
$4,030.00	8	1
$11,000.00	20 (5 days x 4)	1
$3,000.00	3	1
$4,300.00	6	1
$8,000.00	18	1
$7,600.00	20	1
$4,200.00	8	1
$5,250.00	12	1
$6,000.00	8	2
$13,000.00	44	1
$21,225.00	44	12
$13,000.00	33	n/a
$7,000.00	19	n/a
$8,500.00	22	1
$14,000.00	4	14

All of these current amounts should give you a good idea on how much you can make on a single study and how many days it would take to make it.

Either way you look at it, medical studies pay more than your average JOB (just over broke). The average American makes around $15 an hour, which equates to $600 a week. After taxes, insurance, union dues, etc., that will be reduced to about $450 a week, or $1,800 a month. You can make $1,800 in less than a week with the average medical study. Also, if you're doing a longer study, you can also look at the money that you are saving by being in a study. I spend about $30 a day on food ($10 for breakfast, $10 for lunch, and $10 for dinner), not to mention gas, so if I did a twenty-day study, that's $600 I saved just on food (20 days x $30 a day on food) because the facility provides all your meals.

Also, let's face it, the great American Dream that has long been sought after is quickly becoming the American Nightmare for millions of US citizens. In many situations, you're unemployed or underemployed regardless of your educational status. Even if you've been employed your entire life starting from 2020 till 2060, you'll fall into something now known as the 40/40/40 club, which simply means working 40 hours a week for 40 years and then having to live on 40% of your income for retirement. And after all that, you'll probably have nothing more than a house that you still owe on, a car or two, and outstanding credit card bills, etc.

Now I'm certainly not saying that doing a medical study will alleviate all these problems, but I know that people have dreams and aspirations of owning their own little business or doing other things with their life other than working for someone else. There's always two things that seem to block this and that is time and money (lump sum). That's the advantage of doing medical studies. Also, did you know that 63% of Americans don't have enough savings to cover a $500 emergency! Lastly, the sad fact is that a lot of employers will pay you $15-20/hour to forget about your dreams of owning your own business and will never pay you enough to be their neighbor!

And now with COVID-19, things have gotten way worse. We're now seeing huge unemployment numbers and very soon there's set to be massive evictions all across America if a relief bill isn't signed. Which as of this current moment it hasn't. Some people have no idea where their next dollar is coming from and where they are gonna lay their heads at night. Things are getting terrible, but I'm providing a way for you to get a sizable amount of money that could cover you and your family for a few months.

One of the good things about medical studies is that you can pick and choose any study that you might be interested in as long as you fit the criteria or requirements. Women have been included more often into the protocol for studies in the last few years. I say this because in the beginning it was mainly just for males or women who were not child-bearing capable. Lately, there has been an increase in women getting accepted into clinical trials, and some trials have either exclusively wanted women or wanted a certain amount of women.

There is one huge thing to consider that will automatically exclude any potential participant: age. You could be over age or underage, so you should take this into consideration. The average age criteria for most clinical trials is between 18 and 45 or 55 years old. It's never under 18 (unless it's a child study), but there are studies that go up to 65 and I have also seen senior studies that have no age cap.

There are other things to be mindful of, as they could be automatic disqualifications for participating in a specific study. I will get into this as well as other important things that a potential study participant should be aware of. But I can honestly say that I can't think of a better, more lucrative way for the average person who is broke or has little money and skill to make extra (legal) money.

I would also like to add that I have personally done studies with plenty of people who had their college degrees (Associate's/Bachelor's), a few others having their Master's/Doctorate degrees and also quite a few stockbrokers and day traders. So it's not just a bunch of losers that are in this field of work. There are people from all walks of life who found themselves here, and most of them will admit that clinical trials saved their lives. I have hundreds of stories on how studies have saved many people from some difficult financial situations. Some about to be evicted, some needing money to get an apartment or Christmas gifts, others needing to buy a much-needed vehicle for transportation, etc. I can go on and on with these stories, but I'm sure most people reading this have their own stories and can imagine what others have been through.

And speaking of school, this is the perfect situation for someone who is taking online classes because you have so much free time to dedicate to school. A perfect example of someone who took advantage of clinical studies (money and free time) is a person by the name of Robert Rodriguez. Robert is an American filmmaker/screenwriter who directed the 1992 action film *El Mariachi*, which was a commercial success after grossing $2 million against only a $7,000 budget. The money to produce this film came from medical studies. This film also spawned two sequels. Rodriquez has worked with the great filmmaker Quentin Tarantino and currently owns his own cable television channel, El Rey. There are other success stories, but if this isn't enough to prove that great things can happen from the proceeds of medical studies, then I don't know what is.

Another great benefit to medical studies is the free blood lab work that every possible participant will get. These labs will tell you everything you need to know about the health of your body. Almost every vital blood reading will be taken. It lets you know the average human range and your specific readings. It will even detail to you what is high and what is low, if applicable. This blood work can be very pricey and could range anywhere from $100 for just one simple blood test to $3,000 for several complex tests. But on average, the price for most patients is somewhere in the range of $1,500, that you would be getting for free every time you went to screen for a particular medical study.

There's another huge advantage to doing medical studies that I have not mentioned and that is: placebos!! A placebo is a harmless medication, pill or procedure that is given more for the psychological effects than the physical benefits. So a subject can do a $5,000 study basically for free because they would not have taken any real medication, just have to go through the procedures that the other subjects have to (blood draws, physical, etc). Usually one out of four will get the placebo if it's provided in that particular study.

I would also like to say that unlike all the get-rich-quick schemes we all see online like, become wealthy off of real estate, get rich off the stock market, etc., which all require money or a skill, that wouldn't be a prerequisite in the world of clinical trials. With most of those, you need good to great credit to purchase a house; you also need a decent down payment, not to mention closing costs and a bunch of other hidden fees, easily totaling over $15k. For most get-rich-quick schemes or financial freedom programs, you need something that's not easily obtainable to the masses to fully complete, be successful, or make any money doing whatever it is that they are trying to sell you on. But with *Prospering In A Pandemic,* all you need is decent health and you're going to make money - *soon!* It's just that simple. And even if you're not in good health, there are always companies that are in need of people with an existing ailment, high blood pressure, high cholesterol, cigarette smokers or a particular illegal drug user to test.

And lastly, I would like to add that now we're in the age of Covid, everyone wants to get tested which can get tricky or even expensive for those who don't meet the free testing criteria. Well, in comes another advantage to medical studies because almost all (if not all) pharmaceutical clinics are now testing each and every subject as well as staff multiple times for the Coronavirus throughout the duration of that study. Not only are they swabbing the nose, they are taking bloodwork to test for antibodies to look for traces of it to see if you've ever came in contact with the virus. This alone is a huge incentive just to screen for a study, and some locations are even paying $50-$100 every time they do a Covid test on you. They're also going through great lengths with social distancing while staying in the facility with extra spacing of subjects, mandatory masks, etc.

SCREENING

The screening process is the initial step into participating in a medical study. Screening is basically used to see if you are eligible to take part in a particular study. There are certain guidelines that are required to qualify. When screening for a clinical trial, one would have to fall within very specific criteria in order to be chosen for a study, which consists of, but is not limited to:

- informed consent
- medical history
- vital signs (blood pressure)
- EKG/ECG
- height and weight (BMI)
- bloodwork
- drug screening
- temperature
- physical

Whenever you decide to make a screening appointment, an initial phone call is usually needed for this process. The phone screener will ask you a series of questions to determine if you would pre-qualify to participate in the study. If you pass the phone screening, the next process will be to set up a screening date. On your screening date, most of the above things will be performed.

Informed consent: This will be all paperwork that will explain what the study is about in its entirety. This is a contract that will tell you what drug you will be taking, the side effects, the amount (mg), how many doses, the drug sponsor, the lead doctor, compensation, etc. This will determine if you want to continue with this particular study because because you will not want to participate in every study.

Also, another bit of advice I would give is to try to remember key words and information in the consent form, such as the name of the drug they are testing, some of the side effects, how long the study is, etc. I say this because a lot of the time you will get quizzed later by the doctor or the consenter to see if you were listening and read your paperwork.

Medical history: You will be asked a long series of questions about your medical history, including childhood injuries, diseases, allergies, surgeries, etc. The information that you give on this day will follow you forever and be on your permanent record. Make sure this is what you really want them to know because this could determine your eligibility for this study and all future studies at this facility (less unimportant information provided might be beneficial to you). The reason why I say the less "unimportant" information the better is because a lot of people screening love to give their entire life story, like I scraped my knee when I was five or I had a slight cold seven months ago, which is unnecessary to disclose. All major diseases, illnesses, and medical procedures should definitely be reported!

Vital signs: Better known as "blood pressure," vital signs are your essential body functions, including your heartbeat, breathing rate, and temperature. The nurse/tech may watch, measure, or monitor your vital signs to check your level of physical functioning health.

Normal vital signs change with age, sex, weight, exercise capability, and overall health.

Normal vital sign ranges for the average healthy adult while resting are:

- Blood pressure: 120 systolic (top number), 80 diastolic (bottom number)
- Breathing: 12 to 18 bpm
- Pulse (heart rate): 60 to 100 bpm
- Temperature: 97.8 F to 99.1 F

Those are the normal ranges, but in medical studies the cut-off range is usually:

- Blood pressure: 140 systolic (top number), 90 diastolic (bottom number)
- Pulse: 40 to 100 bpm
- Temperature: 98.5

EKG/ECG: This is the painless process of recording electrical activity of the heart over a small period of time using electrodes placed on the skin. Electrodes are usually ten small plastic/metal leads that are connected to thin wires placed on the patient's arms, legs, and across the left side of the chest. Normally the patient lays flat on a bed for about five minutes. The test begins with the tech pressing the start button on the EKG machine, and the reading of the patient will come out in the form of thin paper. A doctor assesses the results at a later time.

Height/weight (BMI): When you go to a screening, you will be weighed and your height will be taken. This is to ensure that you are not over/underweight. This is what is called your BMI (body mass index), which is a measurement of body fat based on height and weight that applies to both men and women between the ages of 18 and 65 years old.

BMI can be used to indicate if you are overweight, obese, underweight or normal. A healthy BMI score is between 20 and 25. A score below 20 indicates that you may be underweight and a value above 25 may indicate that you are overweight. But normally, in medical studies, acceptable ranges are 18 to 32, but other times 30 max and weigh at least 110 lbs. I've also known of rare studies that only went up to 25 and I have seen studies that only accepted participants who had a BMI over 25. In either case, if you are out of range you would automatically disqualify for that particular study.

Bloodwork: A potential participant almost always has to give blood before he or she can be deemed healthy enough to participate in a specific study. Bloodwork consists of a laboratory analysis performed on a blood sample (two or more tubes) that is usually extracted from a vein in the arm using a needle (after fasting for four to eight hours). Many tests are being done in this process. One of the main things that will be tested for is Hepatitis, HIV, and AIDS. If you have any one of these and you are screening for a healthy study, you will be automatically disqualified and that facility will more than likely call your local health department and report this.

The other things they usually test for are:

- WBC (white blood cells)
- RBC (red blood cells)
- Hemoglobin
- Platelets
- Potassium
- Calcium
- Bilirubin
- Cholesterol (Triglycerides)
- HDL (good cholesterol)
- LDL (bad cholesterol)
- Iron
- LFT (liver functions)
- and many more

Some of these results are not as important as others, and if you're not too far out of range you may still be considered for the study (or asked to repeat that specific lab). In most cases, the best labs will be the greatest thing in determining whether or not one makes it into a study over someone else.

Drug screening: Most medical study facilities do a drug screen. This drug screen is usually done through the urine, also known as a urine drug screen or UDS. It's quick and painless. This test screens for alcohol, amphetamines, benzodiazepines, marijuana, cocaine, PCP, and opioids (narcotics). Most facilities also test for alcohol, which is usually done using a breathalyzer. A breathalyzer is a small machine that a person blows into that reads their alcohol level.

If either test reads positive or the numbers are out of order, you will immediately be disqualified from participating in that study. And if it comes out positive for drugs, there is a great chance that you will be banned from ever coming back to that facility to do a medical study, especially if it's something harder than marijuana or alcohol.

Note: it is not wise to eat bagels with poppy seeds, as it is known to show up in drug screenings as a narcotic.

Physical: Lastly, on screening day there is usually a physical, which is done by the doctor of that facility. This physical is brief and consists of checking your heartbeat and lungs using a stethoscope. Other things a doctor might require you to do is walk a straight line, hold your arms out and touch your nose with one finger, follow his finger using only your eyes, and you may have to remove some of your outer layers of clothing to check for rashes, etc. Most people don't fail physicals, but it does happen from time to time.

After screening, there is usually about a week to a month until check-in (blood labs are usually only good for 30 days max). Prior to checking in, the clinic will call you with your results from screening, which could be one of three options. Pass, fail, or repeat. If you pass, the clinic will invite you to participate in the study. If you fail, they will let you know why and the search for another study process begins again. Then there is something called "repeats." Repeat is when one or more of your blood labs, urine, etc., is not within protocol range. When this happens, you have to come back to that facility to give more blood or urine to repeat what was not correct. If certain labs are too far out of range, you automatically fail and will not be allowed to participate in that particular study. There are also cases when labs are too far out of range and you are asked to go see your personal doctor and get outside bloodwork done before you can return to that particular clinic.

Something to remember is to show up to all of your appointments early. Whether it's screening, check-in, o/p (outpatient visit) or repeats. Every clinic has heard every excuse in the book from getting lost, to traffic, to my kids, etc. These will not be sufficient excuses. A lot of this data is very time-sensitive and sometimes even seconds can throw things off. Try to be at least 30 minutes to a full hour early. If you cannot make it to of any of these, CALL THE CLINIC!!! No show, no call is definitely not a good look, and some clinics such as Pfizer will automatically ban you for this, but most have a two to three strike policy with a suspension then a permanent ban.

O/p (outpatient) visits are when you have to return to the clinic after you have finished your main inpatient stay and checked out. You can have several o/p's and they can have a short or long range of time in between. Most subjects (participants) try to avoid studies with o/p's or choose the ones with fewer o/p's. Try to pick the studies that have o/p's that are not spread that far apart, because it makes the study drag on forever, and if you live far from the clinic, you have to make multiple trips back and forth, which can dig into your profit.

Also, most studies have a 30-day wash out period, which means that you have to wait 30 days from the time you finish one study to check into another study (for your safety). It all depends on the specific study and the clinic itself. Some clinics require that you wait

30 days from the time you last dosed (took the drug) and some will require that you wait at least 30 days from the last day of the complete study, even if the last day was an o/p day, which can delay your next eligibility to do another study at that facility for a few weeks or even months. It's an anomaly but not super rare to see a 60-day, 90-day or even longer washout period, which most subjects avoid because it cripples you from participating in another study for so long.

There is now something that a lot of facilities have implemented into their system and that is VCT. VCT is an acronym for Verified Clinical Trials – a verification system that some facilities use to determine if a subject has participated/screened at another facility within 30 days of screening/participating at another. There are different penalties for this. Some facilities will just tell you that you did not come in verified because you were just at another clinic and you would have to leave. Others such as Pfizer might ban or suspend you for this offense. So be aware and mindful of this before screening. I will list the facilities later in another chapter that have VCT, but double-check because this verification could be added at any time by a company. Also, some facilities will fingerprint you at every screening, this is their method of VCT (this has absolutely nothing to do with the law). And lastly, most facilities that have VCT don't want you to even screen at two different clinics within the same time frame (30 days), so ask questions and be aware!

Most medical research facilities do not share your vital information, just your VCT, so you don't have to worry about confidentiality. As a matter of fact, the only time this is done is if that particular facility has multiple locations. Example: Icon Clinical Trials has three different locations: Dallas, Texas; Daytona Beach, Florida; and Madison, Wisconsin. All locations will have your information in their system, even if you only visited or contacted one.

I'm aware that I've mentioned you shouldn't give your entire life story when giving your health history. Again, I'm certainly not saying don't disclose any illness, diseases, etc., that you might have. You should definitely tell the interviewer all of those things. My point is something as simple as you don't eat pork doesn't have to be disclosed. The majority of studies don't require you to eat the entire meals so there's no need to get disqualified for something as menial as that when you can just simply not eat what you don't want to, while keeping that information to yourself. But something such as being lactose intolerant, as well as other illnesses, should definitely be disclosed.

CHECK-IN

When you have passed screening, you will be asked to come back to the clinic to stay for the amount of time that specific study requires. Each check-in is different for every study facility for the simple fact that each facility has its own procedures, rules, and regulations the participants must abide by. There are things you can do and bring into some clinics that you can't do with others (they will go over all this at screening). Some clinics give you scrubs everyday, while others require you to bring your own clothes. I prefer the clinics with scrubs- less packing.

    Before checking into the facility, there are preparations that you have to make before your arrival. First, you have to find out what you can and can't bring to that specific facility. You have to pack whatever you think you need for that amount of time at that particular clinic. The entire stay at that facility will be completely free room and board. You will be provided with all the necessary bedding, etc., and also breakfast, lunch, and dinner. Most facilities also provide snacks at the end of the night for participants (optional).

I would also suggest you do a few things to give yourself a more competitive chance at making the study. Here's a list:

- Don't exercise, work out, or do any strenuous activities at least five days before checking in/screening.

- Try not to eat greasy, fried, or fatty/fast food about three days prior to check-in/screening.
- Try to pack warm, even in the summer, because most clinics are cold.
    - Sweaters, hoodies, thick socks, long johns, etc.
- Bring your own toiletry items, but keep it simple. Most things we use in everyday life will not be allowed into the clinic.
- Anything that contains aloe, tooth-whitening agents, vitamins, or alcohol will be confiscated and given back at check-out. If you bring something that is not allowed, it will be packed into a plastic bag with your name on it and stored away until the study is over, when it will be returned to you.
- Make sure your packed bag is free of any type of medication, vitamins, gum, candy, food, condoms, etc. These things could get you kicked out of the study before it even begins.
- Here are some things to pack:
    - underwear and socks for the amount of time of your stay (some clinics have washer/dryers)
    - shower slippers
    - things to keep yourself occupied such as X-box, PlayStation, knitting, cell phone, laptop, cards, books, etc., because there's so much downtime.
- Do not drink alcohol at least three days prior to checking-in/screening, as it raises liver enzymes.

- Refrain from rough sex about two days prior to checking-in/screening (possible blood in urine).
- Do not do any street drugs or cigarettes weeks/months prior to checking-in/screening.
- Drink A LOT of water.

A few facilities, due to privacy laws, did not allow camera phones in the past, but the majority do now. Some are more lenient with this than others. They will simply tell you that there will be absolutely no picture taking or recording of any kind. Others will use a small piece of tape to cover the camera part of your phone or laptop camera while others such as Pfizer in New Haven, Connecticut do not allow camera phones at all. I've heard they recently fixed this issue and now allow it. But all of them do allow laptops with cameras, and most will just cover the camera lens.

The actual checking-in process is quite unique because, like I mentioned previously, each facility is different and has their own methods. But one thing they all have in common is when a participant checks in, they're NOT automatically in the study at that point! You still have to re-screen just like you did at your initial screening to qualify again, and if anything is off, you might have to do a repeat or just simply be disqualified from doing that particular study. So it is imperative that your labs be in good range at the point of check-in and screening.

Then there is this little thing that every potential participant dreads hearing, and that is being an "alternate." Alternates are basically back-up participants who would take the place of the main participants if something happens to them. For example, if a particular study needs 10 participants to dose (actually take the medication), most clinics will bring in about 13 or 14 people, which means that they will have about three or four back-ups just in case someone doesn't show up, something goes wrong, or labs come up abnormal with their principal participants. Usually alternates stay one night, and if everything goes right with the main participants, the alternates will go home the next morning after checking in and receive a small stipend, usually anywhere from $100 to $300, but I have seen cases where alternates stayed six days and received $1800 (six days x $300), and they most likely would not have taken any drug at that point. One nice perk to being a alternate is that in many cases some facilities will make you a priority, which will give you almost a guarantee of making it into the next study so long as your labs, vitals, and EKGs are within normal range.

If one of the main participants has issues such as high blood pressure, bad labs, etc., they would use an alternate to take that participant's place. That participant would go home and get paid alternate's pay. Don't be discouraged at being an alternate, because in almost every study, at least one alternate has made it in. I have seen studies where all the alternates have made it in. Also I would like to add that I have witnessed dozens of studies where there wasn't any alternates. In this case, everyone automatically made it in if their labs were within range.

What makes you an alternate can have many variations, such as:

- You had a repeat at screening.
- You had to repeat your check-in labs.
- You screened on the last day of screening. Example: if that particular study is screening on three separate days, it's best to screen on the first or second day because the third day will either result in you being at the end of the participants list or an alternate.
- When you screened, you showed up last on screening day. Try to be one of the first few people when screening, even on the first or only day of screening.
- They simply had enough people and you ended up an alternate.
- And lastly, a lot of clinics will tell you that at check-in that everyone is an alternate until you dose (take the drug).

All of these scenarios can and will happen to you at least once in your study career, so don't get discouraged by this. You will more than likely win more than you will lose if you're in decent health.

There is a saying in the study community, "Don't pay that bill until you take that pill." 😉

THE STUDY

So you screened, checked in, and successfully passed both. Congrats. You're in the study! Now there are endless sequences of events that could happen throughout different studies, but I will take you through how the average study would normally flow.

When you initially check in, there are a few things that have to be done. The first is change into scrubs (if that clinic provides scrubs) or have your bags and pockets checked. You also give blood, have an EKG, get weighed, maybe have a physical, and then eat lunch and dinner. Most times, in between lunch and dinner, there's a quick meeting giving you a brief overview of the study and maybe a small tour or description of the facility, mainly for the participants who have never been to that clinic before. After dinner, there's always a few hours left to relax, socialize with the other participants, shower, and get ready for the next day, which is usually a very busy day.

The busy days (usually at least one) are called PK days. PK is short for Pharmacokinetics, which is basically determining the effects of substances given to a living organism. With clinical trials, the substance of interest is usually pharmaceutical drugs that need to be tested. The main reason for this is to analyze the drug's metabolism and safety in the body from the moment that it enters the body until it is completely eliminated from the body.

PK days usually involve a lot of blood draws, in which blood will be extracted from the body into a small tube. This is done in either of two ways:

Straight stick: This is the most common method when it comes to taking blood samples. Samples are taken from a vein using a regular standard needle the same way you probably had done when you gave blood in the past.

Peripheral venous catheter: also known as just a catheter, is a small, flexible tube that is placed into the vein in order to administer or extract medication, blood or fluids. This method is often preferred by subjects than straight sticks in clinical trials, especially on PK days, because you won't have to keep getting stuck with a straight stick needle. The catheter remains in the vein for around 24 hrs for blood and the vacutainer (blood tube with a vacuum) is simply inserted into the catheter and the blood is automatically sucked into the tube.

During your PK day, which is usually the second day in, you will most likely do a series of vital signs, EKG's, and blood draws throughout the day. You will most likely get up very early that morning because there are plenty of things to do.

I'm basing this mock study on a standard ten-day study. Like I mentioned earlier, the first day will most likely be settling in and finding out who actually made it into the study and who didn't (from bloodwork, EKG's, vitals, etc.). That announcement will usually be made the next morning during PK day. The chosen subjects will stay and the alternates will go home. You will most likely go through the majority of these events during the earlier part of the morning and afternoon; it usually slows down towards the evening.

The next few days usually are not that busy, and you will get maybe one or two blood draws a day and maybe an EKG or vitals taken. The other days outside of PK day will be mostly eating (breakfast, lunch, dinner, and an optional snack). Some facilities require that you eat ALL of your food while some require at least 75% of it. Others require that you only eat all your food during PK days and the rest of the clinics have no rules at all about eating (you can eat some or none of your food, your choice). You will have a lot of downtime to do as you please, within the clinic's rules and regulations.

Also, all throughout the study you will be asked a lot about any A/E's. A/E is an acronym for Adverse Effect, which is basically an unwanted, harmful effect resulting from medication, drugs, surgery, or anything that can be deemed harmful or even helpful to the body. A/E is also known as side effects. You will be asked at least once a day how you are feeling, do you have any pain, etc. You have to inform them of any deviations to your body, from something as small as a headache or a rash to extreme pain.

You cannot leave the facility for any reason unless they decide to take your group out for fresh air. Visitors are not allowed, only in the case of coming to bring a subject something they forgot, so long as it is allowed by the clinic (it will be inspected by the staff).

A subject can drop out of a study at any given time and for any reason. You would be prorated the protocol pay for what you did up to that time (usually losing your completion bonus). All facilities will tell you that they won't hold it against you, but I can tell you from experience that it is not a good thing to do and it will definitely go against you in some way (unless it was for obvious health reasons).

In this hypothetical ten-day study, there is a decent chance that you will get another PK day (busy day) toward the end of the study. When the study gets to the tenth day, that morning you will most likely give blood, take an EKG test, get your vitals checked, and complete a physical. After all of that is done, you will have your bags rechecked (to make sure you haven't taken anything that doesn't belong to you) and you exit the clinic. Now you are free.

I would say at least 90% of the clinics have a check (or their form of payment) for you when you leave, while others mail it to you. If you did receive a check, it would not be for the total amount the majority of the time. There could be a few reasons for this. First, you could have an o/p in which you would have to come back to the facility for another blood draw, etc. In that case, they would probably give you another check at that time. Or you could have a follow-up phone call in which they will ask you how you're feeling and after that they would mail you the remainder of your money. Also, many clinics are starting to give participants their pay on a debit card and, after these events are completed, the money is uploaded to the card.

The breakdown would probably go something like this. Let's say the study is ten days with one o/p visit a week later. On average, that would be a $3,500 study (ten days x $300 a day + $100 for the follow-up visit + $400 completion bonus). The clinic would probably give you around $2,500 when you leave on the last day (tenth day) and when you return, they would give you a check for the remaining $1,000. In the old days, early 2000s and before, from what I've been told they used to give you all the money at the end of your first stay, but many subjects wouldn't return for the rest of the study so they stopped doing that and started withholding the money until you completed the entire study.

That's basically how an average study will go. Of course, there are many different variables that could change this format drastically. There are so many different types of studies that you can do and each one is different. MRI studies are a totally different animal than, let's say, a spinal tap study or even just a normal standard study that I just used as an example.

But for the most part, the ten-day study that I described is the way I would say 70% of studies would go. Unless they are specialties like I just gave examples of (MRI, etc), which many of those are single-person studies not groups (multiple-person) studies. But pretty much, no matter what the study is, most of them have the same basic core elements.

**There's something that I'm just being made aware of that has been added by a few facilities, Abbvie in Waukegan/Chicago, Illinois, and ICON in Lenexa/Kansas City, Kansas, in particular. I mentioned the VCT system being added at some facilities, and I know that I said that it was only for identifying whether or not a subject has participated at another clinic, but those two facilities have taken it a step further. They now use it for participation intel plus they run a criminal background and check to see if you're on a sex offenders list or under any type of supervision (probation/parole). Those are the only two facilities that I'm aware of that do this, but others can add it at any time, so keep that in mind if any of this applies to you.

LESS RISK/STAY HEALTHY

I am very aware that there is one big concern that many people interested in clinical trials are going to have, and that is vaccines! I understand this unsettling feeling that many have, but I can honestly tell you that you can have a successful study career without ever doing a vaccination-type study. I know plenty who have done it. And the fact of the matter is the mass majority of medical studies are not vaccines.

Speaking of vaccines and all the pros/cons of them, anyone who was in favor of them or even has doubts about them could've easily done a medical study and gotten paid to take the Covid vaccine. I know of a few pharmaceutical facilities that were conducting the Coronavirus vaccine test but one in particular was paying $10,000 per participant to do so. Not only would you have been making good money and receiving the same or close to the same vaccination as everyone else, but you would be closely monitored for a year or so, letting you know if even one of your blood test levels was slightly off. This is something that the majority of the public who has taken the vaccination doesn't have the privilege of knowing or receiving.

There are plenty of things that you can do to your advantage or take less risk when doing clinical trials. But if I had to pick the number one way to do this, I would say that it would simply be to just pick the studies that are safer and work better for you. I have seen and heard of studies that I would never participate in, regardless of how good the money is. Here is a brief list of the type of studies that I personally would not participate in, but I know people who have (and they still do studies). This is my semi-expert opinion:

- Anything that may result in permanent damage to the brain (strong psychiatric medications/drugs)
- Spinal taps (needle in the back)
- Anything that has to specifically do with the heart (permanent/prolonged damage)
- Anything that has severe/permanent liver damage
- Anything that has a high rate of tumor growth
- Anything with a high rate of any permanent negative results
- Pick-line studies (small tube inserted that usually runs from the inner forearm to your heart)

I personally know people who've done each and every one of those studies that I just mentioned and most of them had little or no health issues when they did; it was just my choice or preference not to participate in them. Also, I would simply say: use your better judgment when searching for a study. Money is always a big factor for picking a study, but use common sense, be smart, and be picky. Just because the money is good doesn't mean you don't have to beware. What's the sense in doing a study for $10k if the side effects are so bad that it permanently damages your body to the point where one or more labs show up out of range forever and you may never qualify for another study again? So be wise, my fellow subjects, and always do your due diligence!

There are always plenty of studies going on (especially if you're willing to travel), so don't feel pressured into doing one that you're not comfortable with. And don't always go for the one with the largest payout because not only might it not be good for your health but the competition is usually higher because of the monetary incentive.

For example: there was a $15k West Nile Virus study out a few year ago that lasted an entire year (they actually inject you with the virus). But instead of doing that one, you could have done six (one every other month) $5k studies and made $30k that year, with way less health risk.

But back to staying healthy, I can tell you one thing, even if you don't make it into any studies that you screened for, you will get to know your body just from the screenings. You will learn if you have any heart problems, if you have high blood pressure, if you have any liver problems, etc. You will also learn a lot of the terminology for medical issues as well. Basically you could become very educated on your body, and health in general, for free.

I will list below a few common things that could potentially exclude you from participating in a study. Not only will I list the ailment, I will also list a few things that you can do to possibly correct this problem.

High blood pressure: This is one of the most common roadblocks that I have seen people in the study game have. It knocks a lot of people out during screening and even more during check-in. There is something called white-coat syndrome, which means that when a subject is about to get their vitals done (especially after check-in), they get very nervous because they realize that this is the only thing that stands between them getting potentially thousands of dollars or going home broke, and they just can't get past someone in a white coat or a tech in scrubs putting that blood-pressure cuff on them. As soon as they feel the cuff getting tighter, their heart starts racing, which, in turn, raises their blood pressure and heart rate.

Many subjects who fail this don't even have high blood pressure. It's just that they might be borderline and get scared at that moment to the point where they can't help how their body reacts. And I can guarantee you, if a lot of them took their blood pressure any other time, they would pass. In these cases, you just have to put yourself in a position where you are comfortable and confident that you will pass every time because your numbers are on the lower end and have room to play with. Also, your blood pressure is lowest when you are laying down (supine), than sitting, and highest when standing.

There are a few things you could do to prevent high blood pressure or the fear of your pressure being high when you're getting your vitals taken. Here is a list of things that you can do or take:

Garlic – Garlic is one of the simplest things to take for high blood pressure. It can be taken in many different forms. Pill (preferably gel) form is probably the easiest way to consume it because all you need is water. You can purchase garlic pills at many places such as major grocery stores, Walmart, health stores, GNC, The Vitamin Shoppe, etc. They are best taken in the morning on an empty stomach because it makes for a very powerful natural antibiotic. It is more effective before breakfast because bacteria is exposed and cannot defend itself from the power of the garlic. Also, some people claim that consuming garlic on an empty stomach is a very good remedy for nerve problems, which is great for reducing high blood pressure.

Garlic is good for people who suffer from hypertension. It also prevents heart problems and aids in proper functioning of the liver and bladder, as well as being effective for circulation. It is effective for stomach problems, like diarrhea.

You can incorporate garlic into cooking when you're making meals. Not only is it still effective, it also adds a good flavor to your food. But anyway, if you decide to consume garlic, just know that it is a very good addition to your overall health. **For study protocol, stop taking pills anywhere from one week to a month before screening or checking into a study. That's the usual allotted time but do your due diligence on that study's specifics.

Apple cider vinegar – ACV is very rich in antioxidants. High blood pressure puts a lot of strain on the walls of your arteries. But the antioxidant that can be found in ACV can help to heal this. ACV is also a very good detoxifying agent. The walls of the arteries harden with plaque formation as you age. People who lead an unhealthy lifestyle and/or those with prior health conditions have much greater plaque buildup. The detoxifying effect of ACV helps to flush the blood vessels and somewhat decrease the plaque amount. As a result, your blood vessels allow for smoother and increased blood flow, which helps to reduce blood pressure. If you're not trying to lose weight, you should take ACV moderately because it is also known to be an effective weight loss tool. **For study protocol, stop using anywhere from a week to a month before screening or actually checking into a study. That's the usual allotted time but again do your due diligence on that study specifics.

Other things you can do to help with high blood pressure include:

- Limit your salt intake
- Maintain a healthy weight
- Stop tobacco use
- Moderate alcohol intake
- Get plenty of quality sleep
- Manage stress
- Breath deeply (take up breathing exercises)
- Yoga
- Cardio is your best friend!!!! Nothing strenuous as far as lifting. This will raise your muscle enzymes, unless your body is used to it. Running, jogging, biking, any of those elliptical-type of gym machines that raise your heart rate can be helpful, but stop a few days before screening or checking in because you wouldn't want it to raise your muscle enzymes.
- Power walks

- Fruits (orange juice, bananas, cantaloupe, honeydew melon, dried fruits such as prunes and raisins, etc.)
- Vegetables (ones that are rich in potassium: potatoes, kidney beans, peas, sweet potatoes, tomatoes, etc.)
- Dark chocolate
- Switch to decaf coffee
- Tea (decaf)
- Relax
- Try to cook with 100% real olive oil or 100% coconut oil as much as possible as opposed to vegetable oil.

There are more ways to reduce blood pressure, but those are the major ways to see results. After a while of trial and error, you will find what's best for your body.

High CPK levels – CPK levels are tested to find damage to the muscles, including the heart muscles. Creatine kinase (CK) is an enzyme found in the muscles. Enzymes are proteins that help the body's cells do their job. The level of CK enzymes rises when you have damage to the muscle cells in your body.

This rise can come from multiple things, but it usually comes from lifting something heavy or lifting and exercising when your body isn't used to that type of strain. It can also be inflated from things other than lifting, such as acute muscle injury or a chronic disease.

A normal CPK range level in the human body is anywhere from 22 to 198 U/L and it's not rare for medical studies to accept subjects up to 279. I have known subjects who exercised (push-ups) while in a study, and one in particular's levels went all the way up to 6600 from just doing 100 push-ups. This extreme increase will only happen if your body isn't used to it. For example: I know a subject who did about 150 push-ups one morning (while participating in a study) and wasn't aware that staff were taking safety labs that same morning. They took the necessary blood test and his labs did not increase enough for a repeat or for them to ask any questions. This is only because he works out all the time and his body is used to it.

If you find yourself in a predicament that you feel you might have high CPK levels from lifting something heavy or exercising, there are a few things you could do to help with this problem.

- Avoid strenuous exercise five to seven days before getting a CPK level test.
- Do warm-ups before doing any high-intensity exercises.
- Lower your blood pressure by reducing your stress levels.
- Get plenty of rest and use ice or heat packs on the target muscle.
- Drink plenty of water.
- Drink 100% cherry juice.
- Drink 100% blueberry smoothies.
- Use cayenne pepper when cooking your food or mix it into a smoothie.
- Eat foods that are known to lower cholesterol, which also prevents heart disease. Heart disease is one of the big reasons for high CPK levels.

- Eat foods such as eggs, fish, brown rice, almonds, and bananas.
- And lastly, cut alcohol out of your diet as much as possible. Drinking alcohol can increase your CPK levels by affecting your muscle tissues. When drinking alcohol, there is stress on the muscle tissue because it is exposed to the alcohol, which increases your CPK levels.

BMI – Many subjects have a problem with their weight, which makes them have an out-of-range BMI (body mass index). You don't necessarily have to be fat or obese to be over the range that a lot of clinical trials are looking for, which is usually around 30-32 max. The average 35-year-old man has a BMI of around 27, so there's not too much wiggle room for a lot of people because the older most people get, the slower their metabolism becomes, which guarantees weight gain. And after a few big meals and no exercise, that could easily go up a few points.

The solution to this is very easy– exercise and watch what you eat and how much. You don't have to kill yourself at the gym, but you should be consistent with doing some sort of exercise at least a few times a week. This should include walking/jogging/running so at minimum you won't gain any more weight, then work on losing a few pounds.

Eating and dieting will probably be the most important and hardest for most people. Starting with the obvious, you should cut back on sugars and starches (any white foods) as much as possible. These are the foods that stimulate secretion of insulin in the body. Insulin is the main fat storage hormone in the human body, so when insulin decreases, fat has an easier time getting out of the fat stores and the body will then burn fats instead of carbs.

Second, eat proteins and vegetables. Each meal should include a protein source and low-carb vegetables. The importance of eating plenty of protein cannot be overstated for the simple fact that it has been shown to boost metabolism by 80 to 100 calories per day. Also, constructing your meals this way will automatically bring your carb intake to a daily recommended 20-50 grams.

Protein sources include:

- Fish and seafood - trout, shrimp, lobster, salmon, etc.
- Meat - chicken, beef, lamb, etc.
- Eggs - organic, Omega-3 enriched or pastured eggs are best

Low-carb vegetables:

- Celery
- Cucumber
- Lettuce
- Swiss chard
- Kale
- Brussels sprouts
- Spinach
- Cauliflower
- Bell peppers
- Asparagus
- Mushrooms

- Zucchini
- Avocados
- Green beans
- Garlic
- Tomatoes
- Radishes
- Onions
- Eggplant
- Cabbage
- Artichokes

I cannot emphasize how much working out is helpful for weight loss, weight maintaining, and overall good health. The best option is to go to the gym about three to four times a week. Lifting weights is very effective for burning calories and preventing your metabolism from slowing down. My suggestion for weight loss would be to lift lighter weights and do more reps because you want to cause a burn and a sweat, which is more effective than lifting heavy with low reps— which is mainly to build strength and muscle.

Cardio is definitely your best friend when trying to lose weight. If you're an amateur or beginner, I would suggest you start out slow and walk maybe a mile or two every day for a few weeks, graduate to jogging, then go to the gym. When you reach the gym stage, keep it mild. A little workout is better than not doing anything at all, and consistency beats out everything!

Low RBC/WBC - Your RBC stands for red blood corpuscles - aka - red blood count and also goes by erythrocytes. In the body, you have a protein called hemoglobin. The blood gets its color when the hemoglobin absorbs oxygen from the lungs. The main function of RBC is for the hemoglobin to release oxygen in the tissues. RBC's have a life cycle of about four months before it recycles itself.

WBC stands for white blood corpuscles – aka – white blood count also known as leukocytes. Your WBC has a totally different function than your RBC. Their main function is to be a defense mechanism of the human body to fight off infections.

Often times, ordinary people have low RBC and/or WBC. Subjects can have this problem because they are giving blood on a constant basis, but there are many other causes for this. Having low or deficient red blood cell counts can cause:

- Trauma
- Kidney disease
- Failure of bone marrow
- Chronic inflammation or other medical conditions
- Feeling faint or weak

Having low white blood cell count can contribute to:

- Colds, viruses, stress, pain, all the way up to HIV/AIDS. The main component of your white blood cells is your body's immune system, so when it is deficient, the body will not be able to properly defend itself from anything attacking it.
- Any autoimmune disorders that attack white blood cells
- Diseases caused by parasites

So as you can see, having proper RBC/WBC levels is important, whether or not you are trying to make it into a medical study. Naturally, when you are participating in medical trials, your blood is on the lower end because whenever you are screening, checking in, and participating in a study, blood is constantly being taken. Fortunately, there are many things you can do to increase your levels and/or get them back to normal range. Below are some of the best ways to do this.

There are foods that will help raise your RBC, which are:

- Lean meats such as beef, chicken, and turkey
- Mussels, clams, and cockles
- Eggs
- Nuts
- Green leafy vegetables such as spinach, broccoli, kale, chard or lamb's lettuce
- Whole grains
- Dried raisins
- Coldwater fish such as salmon or sardines
- Dairy products such as cheese and yogurt (preferably low-fat or skim)
- Mushrooms
- Beer yeast and wheat germ
- Avocado
- Breads and cereals fortified with folic acid
- Citrus fruits such as oranges, grapefruit, lemons, strawberries or kiwi

Foods and vitamins that will help raise your WBC are as follows:

- vitamin A
- Omega-3 fatty acids

- Carotenoids
- Vitamin C
- Green tea
- Selenium
- Zinc
- Vitamin E

Now a lot of the foods and vitamins that I listed above are a very good source and assistance to your daily diet when it comes to healthy WBC/RBC levels. But when you're dealing with the world of clinical trials and you just did a study where they took 500 ml of blood (average amount for a blood donation) and you have another screening soon, you're going to want to get your levels back up as fast and as safely as possible. I'm about to tell you the best way to do this.

There is a supplement that I will not mention here but you can find on our Patreon and Only Fans page under the name, Blood_Money. All of this information along with other helpful tips can be found in the link in the description on the Instagram/Twitter page which is also entitled "Prospering In A Pandemic" and on Facebook which is entitled "Create Wealth With Your Health". But I can give a quick example of how well this supplement works. A friend of mine at the time had completed a study where a decent amount of blood was taken. He had another screening not too long afterwards, so he took this supplement a few days before his screening, two pills that morning and two later that night. After he screened he got back his results informing him that he had too much blood in his body, which clearly lets you know how quick and effective this supplement works.

But, in conclusion, he just simply re-screened for that particular lab reading, which came out fine the second time around and he made it into that study.

So, in conclusion, this would be one of the fastest and safest methods over most others. I know a lot of people would suggest iron pills, but that mainly targets your iron levels and does not totally concentrate on your RBC/WBC. Also, I would recommend drinking "PLENTY" of water because this is a huge aid in blood replacement and replenishment, along with incorporating some of the foods that I previously mentioned.

High AST or ALT levels - These two levels are liver enzymes. AST is the acronym for aspartate aminotransferase, which are muscle enzymes and many other tissues besides the liver but is tested for in liver blood tests. ALT is the acronym for alanine aminotransferase, which is an enzyme exclusively found in the liver.

The reason why liver tests are performed in almost all clinical trials is because the liver is a very important and vital organ. The liver's main job is to filter the blood coming from the digestive tract before passing it to the rest of the body. The liver also detoxifies chemicals and metabolizes drugs and alcohol. When doing so, it secretes bile that ends up back in the large and small intestines. The liver also makes proteins important for blood clotting and other functions. So basically, everything from stress to poisons goes through the liver. It's constantly working and very important to having a healthy body.

Foods that you can eat to aid the liver are:

- Garlic
- Beets and carrots
- Green tea
- Leafy green vegetables
- Avocados
- Apples
- Olive oil
- Alternative grains
- Cruciferous vegetables
- Lemons and limes
- Walnuts
- Cabbage
- Turmeric

Other ways you can take care of your liver are:

- Limit your alcohol intake. Alcohol can damage or destroy the liver cells.
- Try to limit or manage your medication intake.
- Adopt a healthy lifestyle. Eat a healthy diet and exercise regularly.
- Avoid touching or breathing toxins.

There's another supplement that I would incorporate in my diet to assist cleansing the liver out. This supplement I will not mention here but you can find it on our Patreon and Only Fans page under the name, Blood_Money. This supplement is very good for the liver and for gallbladder disorders. It also works as an anti-inflammatory and antioxidant agent. When dealing with medical studies, the use of this particular supplement would mainly be used after drinking alcohol the night before, or prior to taking medication, drugs, smoking or ingesting foreign or harmful substances into your body. * (For study protocol, stop the use in the allotted time frame.)

Colds/Flu - If there is any advice that I would give about colds/flu, it would be to not take any prescription or OTC (over-the-counter) cold medication if you're considering screening or entering a medical study. I made this mistake years ago and paid for it. I rode in a car from New Jersey to South Carolina one year and the AC only worked on high and I caught the worst cold ever. I took normal liquid cold medication (I forgot which one, but they're all basically the same as far as ingredients go). I screened for a study in Baltimore about two weeks later and my labs showed up like I smoked marijuana (cannabis), which I never smoked/used in my life (not even experimented). This caused me to get a six-month ban at that particular clinic.

What I would suggest in this case would be to try to cure this as naturally as possible. Here are a few methods that I would try:

- Hot natural tea (decaf) and real honey (the kind with the honey comb still in the jar)
- Rest as much as possible
- Gargle, preferably warm, seasalt water, or gargle warm water, honey, and apple cider vinegar mixture. Do this about four times a day.
- Drink hot liquids (try to stay hydrated)
- Blow your nose often (rid your body of mucus)
- Stay away from dairy as much as possible
- Take warm/hot steamy showers
- Apply hot or cold packs around your congested sinuses

- Try not to fly if possible
- Sleep with an extra pillow under your head
- There are a few other natural supplements that do wonders against attacking the common cold or flu. I will also add these to our Patreon and Only Fans page.

High Bilirubin – Bilirubin is a yellowish pigment found in bile, a fluid made by the liver. A high level of bilirubin in the blood can lead to jaundice. Jaundice is a yellow color in the skin, eyes, or mucus membranes. Jaundice is normally the main reason to check one's bilirubin levels, and this is often found to be present in newborns. Causes of jaundice vary from non-serious to potentially fatal.

There are prescription drugs on the market to counter high bilirubin and jaundice, which you probably want to stay away from if you're planning on doing a clinical study. Here are a few natural things you can do to help with this ailment:

- Drink about two liters of water a day (purification of toxins and harmful fats)
- Avoid drinking alcohol as much as possible
- Eat nutrient-rich foods: fruits, vegetables, lean sources of protein such as fish, poultry and beans, low-fat dairy, and healthy fats such as olive oil
- Drink a glass of 100% vegetable juice daily
- On an empty stomach, start the day drinking warm tea with a squeezed lemon
- Get as much fiber as possible

I'm gonna teach you one helpful trick you can do to aid you in successfully passing a bilirubin test. This was something that I was educated on by an experienced RN that I worked with for some years. I will not touch on it in this guide, but you can get this information on out Patreon and Only Fans page, as well as other helpful tips.

Out-of-range EKG/ECG – There are so many different variables that come along with an out-of-range EKG/ECG that I won't get too deep into it. I will just give you a few key things that are important to this subject. First, there are plenty of people who are completely healthy but have EKG/ECG's that come up flawed. There are three major things that a person who's not an MD, nurse or medical tech can immediately understand when looking at an EKG/ECG read-out. This is your Range; either it's gonna be Normal, Borderline, or Prolonged. Normal is what you would want to have, but trust me I've witnessed plenty of borderline EKG/ECG readings in which the participant still made it into that particular study.

Another important thing that you want to be in range is your QTC (quantum tunneling composite) level reading. You want your QTC to be under 450, under 400 is even better, but anything over 450 will more than likely disqualify you from most studies, and after too many you might get asked to go see a specialist on your own. Most other readings have to do with your heartbeat pattern (the way it beats) but your QTC has more to do with pressure and resistance, which has more effect on how healthy your heart is than the way it is beating or pumping.

Now, what is the remedy for an out-of-range EKG/ECG? Well, there is no one real answer for that because, like I said, a lot of people who are 100% healthy can have an out-of-range EKG/ECG. Human hearts just beat differently and have a different pattern; that doesn't necessarily mean anything is wrong with you.

So the best answer to a better EKG/ECG reading is simply a healthier heart. The good part about that is there are plenty of things that a person can do to improve the health of their heart. Here are a few important tips you can do to be on your way to a more fit heart:

- Stay as active as possible – any movement is better than none. Take the stairs instead of the elevator or escalator, take walks around the block, park your car further from the store or place that you are going into.
- Join a gym (focus on cardio and abdominal excercises).
- Quitting smoking is a must.
- Eat fish, especially ones that are high in Omega-3 fatty acids (salmon, herring, sardines, tuna).
- Stretch first thing in the morning and practice yoga.
- Moderate red wine is good for your HDL (good cholesterol).
- Stay away from fried food as much as possible.
- Switch to real 100% olive oil or 100% coconut oil when cooking.
- Reduce your salt intake (very important) and switch to sea salt or Himalayan salt.
- If you crave sweets, the best thing to eat is rich, dark chocolate but don't overdo it.

- Vacuuming and mopping are actually very good exercise for an older adult.
- Almonds, walnuts, pecans, and other tree nuts are powerful for lowering the risk of coronary or cardiovascular heart disease.
- Fitness does not have to be boring. You can roller skate or go bowling.
- Ride a bike.
- Reduce your fat intake.

Smokers/Street drug use – This part is very easy. If you smoke ANYTHING, from cigarettes, to marijuana, to cigars, etc., you will automatically be disqualified from any study that you screen for (unless it's a smoking study), if it shows up in your drug screen. The same goes for street drugs. If you take any street drug from cocaine to heroin, etc., you will be automatically disqualified from any study that you screen for (unless that study specifically requires that). Also, I will add that there's a great chance that you will be suspended or banned from ever doing any future studies at that specific clinic.

If any of these are a lifestyle that you partake in, you should investigate how long those specific substances stay in the human body before screening. Each person's body is different and each drug is different, so it's hard to say how long a person should stop for. I would not want to give you wrong information (which might cause you thousands in potential losses) so I suggest that you Google this information because only you know how much you smoke or how much you use certain drugs. All of this has to be calculated in order to determine how long it would take that specific substance not to be detected in your blood or urine. But my overall suggestion would be to just STOP!

Every study will tell you to wait at least 30 days before you participate in another study. I can tell you that the MASS majority of subjects don't abide by this. As a matter of fact, I've known people who have been in three at one time. If you decide to do this, it requires strategy because there are a few things that can stop this from happening. First is the obvious, the days of the study might not match up. Second, if any of the medications you're taking is a drug (narcotic) it won't work because when it's time to screen or check in to the next study, that drug will show up in the drug screen. And third, if at least two of the clinics you are screening at has VCT, it won't work because they will know that you have attempted to do multiple screenings.

A lot of people have concerns with doing multiple studies at one time for health reasons, which is very understandable. But I can tell you without hesitation that I have seen dozens of subjects do this plenty of times. This takes strategy, your due diligence and precaution in order to be successful and safe at this. I'm certainly not condoning doing multiple studies simultaneously, concurrently or at the same time, I'm just giving the realities of it. Also doing this has gotten harder due to the implementation of VCT, which a lot of study facilities have added to their database.

One thing that I would like to add that would probably be an asset to doing medical studies is that not all studies involve ingesting pills or actual medication. I've witnessed quite a few studies in which subjects only had to drink an alcoholic beverage to test the effects on the body. And I've also seen plenty in which only a cream was involved which would get rubbed on you to see if there was any effects such as rashes, dryness, etc. A few of my buddies are currently in both types of these studies (Nov 2021) and the stipends are $5,700 for the alcohol study and $8,500 for the cream study respectively.

The last thing I would like to add is, some of the things I mentioned above are for everyday use and should be added into your daily diet. Mostly the food fits into the category of daily consumption, while others I would only use when trying to make it into a particular study.

** I'm aware that I mentioned a few supplements that would aid you with your clinical study pursuit. But be aware that most clinics as well as their sponsors want you to stop the use of most supplements within a time frame of about two weeks to 30 days before screening and check-in. Yes, the vast majority of these supplements would not show up in blood labs but it is your responsibility to take them or not within study protocol allotment!

Lastly, I would like to add that out of everything that was mentioned, the best advice that I would give to everyone is make WATER your best friend! I cannot overemphasise how important water is. I tell everyone to try their best to remove all other beverages from your diet (besides 100% juices) or better yet juice or blend your own fruits and vegetables. Drink natural spring water and plenty of it!

LIST OF CLINICAL FACILITIES

This is one of the most important parts: the names and locations of all the major clinical facilities. I will only list the major facilities. I will also give a small description, rating, and what amenities to expect at each specific location. Your geographical location plays a lot into your earning potential when it comes to clinical trials. Some areas of the US are more lucrative than others.

Below is a list of the larger study facilities that are worth visiting (over $1,000 stipend). I included a rating system based on a scale of 1 to 5 (5 being the best), whether scrubs are provided or you have to bring your own clothing, if you can bring a camera phone into that facility, how good the food is, if you can wash your clothes (or if they wash them for you) or have no washer/dryer at all, if they have Wi-Fi, and probably best of all how the pay is. Things change often and new facilities open while old ones close or get bought out by another pharma company, so this information is not set in stone but it's a very good route to get started. Here is the list:

(Facilities with an asteric have VCT.)

State	Facility	Scrubs	Cam phone	Food	Washer /Dryer	Wi-fi	Pay	Rating
Arizona	Celerion* in Tempe, AZ (Phoenix) (866) 445-7033 *VCT	Yes	Yes	3.8	They wash your clothes for you	Yes	3.8	3.5

State	Facility	Scrubs	Cam phone	Food	Washer /Dryer	Wi-fi	Pay	Rating
California	Altasciences LA in Cypress, CA (714) 252-0700	n/a	n/a	n/a	n/a	n/a	n/a	n/a
California	Parexel in Glendale, CA (877) 617-8839 (*They only accept CA residents)	Yes	Yes	n/a	Yes	Yes	5	n/a
California	Anaheim Clinical Trials LLC Anaheim, CA (714)774-7777	n/a	n/a	n/a	n/a	n/a	n/a	n/a
Connecticut	Pfizer* in New Haven, CT (203) 401-0100 *VCT	Yes	Yes	4.5	Yes	Yes	4.5	4.5
Connecticut	INDD in New Haven, CT (203) 401-4300	n/a	n/a	n/a	n/a	n/a	n/a	4.2
Florida	LabCorp in Daytona Beach, FL (386) 366-6400	No	Yes	3.5	Yes	Yes	4	4
Florida	Clinical Pharmacology of Miami. Miami, FL (305) 817-2900	n/a	n/a	n/a	n/a	n/a	n/a	n/a
Florida	Quotient Sciences, Miami (305) 644-9903	n/a	n/a	n/a	n/a	n/a	n/a	3
Florida	OCRC in Orlando, FL (407) 240-7878	n/a	n/a	n/a	n/a	n/a	n/a	n/a
Florida	PPD. Orlando, FL (689) 216-3100	n/a	n/a	n/a	n/a	n/a	n/a	2
Florida	Riverside Clinical Research Edgewater, FL (386) 428-7730	n/a	n/a	n/a	n/a	n/a	n/a	n/a
Florida	FXM Clinical Research of Miramar Miramar, FL (954) 430-1097	n/a	n/a	n/a	n/a	n/a	n/a	n/a
Florida	Miami Clinical Research Miami, FL (305) 433-6496	n/a	n/a	n/a	n/a	n/a	n/a	n/a
Florida	Accord Clinical Research Port Orange, FL (386) 760-7272	n/a	n/a	n/a	n/a	n/a	n/a	n/a
Illinois	AbbVie in Waukegan, IL (800) 827-2778	Yes	Yes	3	Yes	Yes	4.2	4.7
Kansas	Altrasciences KC Overland Park, KS (913) 696-1601	n/a	n/a	n/a	n/a	n/a	n/a	n/a
Kansas	Analab in Lenexa, KS (913) 221-0421	n/a	n/a	n/a	n/a	n/a	n/a	n/a
Kansas	JCCT in Lenexa, KS (913) 221-0421	n/a	n/a	n/a	n/a	n/a	n/a	n/a

State	Facility	Scrubs	Cam phone	Food	Washer /Dryer	Wi-fi	Pay	Rating
Kansas	ICON* in Lenexa, KS (913) 410-2900 *VCT	Yes	Yes	3.7	Yes	Yes	4	4
Kansas	Vince & A in Overland Park, KS (913) 696-1601	n/a	Yes	n/a	n/a	Yes	4.8	4.5
Kansas	Quintiles in Overland Park, KS (913) 894-5533	No	Yes	3.6	Yes	Yes	3.7	4.5
Maryland	Parexel in Baltimore, MD (667) 210-5300	Yes	Yes	3.5	Yes	Yes	4.5	4
Maryland	Johns Hopkins in Baltimore, MD (410) 955-7283	Yes	Yes	5	Yes	Yes	3.8	4.5
Maryland	Pharmaron* in Baltimore, MD (410) 706-8877 *VCT	Yes	Yes	3.6	Yes	Yes	3.8	4.1
Maryland	NIH in Bethesda, MD (301) 594-0803	n/a	Yes	4.4	n/a	Yes	3.5	4.2
Maryland	Hampton House in Baltimore, MD (410) 955-1622	Yes	Yes	5+	Yes	Yes	3.5	4
Maryland	Walter Reed National Military Medical Center Bethesda, MD (301)295-4000	n/a	n/a	n/a	n/a	n/a	n/a	n/a
Massachusetts	Mass General Brigham in Boston, MA** (857) 282-5370	No	Yes	3.5	No	Yes	3.8	4.3
Michigan	Jasper in Kalamazoo, MI (269) 276-8899	n/a	n/a	n/a	n/a	n/a	n/a	n/a
Minnesota	Prism in St. Paul, MN (651) 641-2900	n/a	n/a	n/a	n/a	n/a	n/a	n/a
Minnesota	AXIS Clinicals USA Dilworth, MN (218)284-2947	n/a	n/a	n/a	n/a	n/a	n/a	n/a
Missouri	BioPharma in Columbia, MO (573) 447-6777	n/a	n/a	n/a	n/a	n/a	n/a	n/a
Missouri	Bio-Kinetic in Springfield, MO (417) 831-2048	n/a	n/a	n/a	n/a	n/a	n/a	n/a
Nebraska	Celerion* in Lincoln, NE (866) 445-7033 *VCT	n/a	Yes	n/a	n/a	n/a	n/a	3.8
Nevada	Novum in Las Vegas, NV (702) 435-3902	Yes	Yes	2	n/a	Yes	1.8	2.3
Nevada	PPD. Las Vegas, NV (877) 773-3707	n/a	Yes	n/a	n/a	Yes	n/a	n/a

**ask for the Clinical Research Dept.– from what I understand they have dozens of studies running– to narrow it down ask them to search for studies over $1,000 stipend.

State	Facility	Scrubs	Cam phone	Food	Washer /Dryer	Wi-fi	Pay	Rating
New Jersey	Biotrial* in Newark, NJ (973) 388-2848 *VCT	No	Yes	4	No	Yes	4	4.4
New Jersey	Inflamax* in Neptune, NJ (888) 989-1808 *VCT	Yes	Yes	4	They wash	Yes	3.7	3.7
New Jersey	Hassman* in Marlton, NJ (856) 753-7335	Yes	Yes	3.8	Yes	Yes	4.3	3.9
New Jersey	Frontage in Secausus, NJ (201) 678-0288 *VCT	No	Yes	3.8	No	Yes	3.7	3.5
New Jersey	Clini Labs* in Eatontown, NJ (646) 215-6400 *VCT	Yes	Yes	3.9	No	Yes	3.9	3.9
New Jersey	TKL in Fairlawn, NJ (201) 587-0500 *VCT	Yes	Yes	4.8	n/a	Yes	4	4.1
New York	CliniLabs* in New York, NY (646) 215-6400 *VCT	Yes	Yes	4.3	They wash	Yes	3.7	3.9
New York	Rockefeller in New York, NY (212) 327-8000	n/a	Yes	3.6	n/a	n/a	2	3.3
North Carolina	Duke in Durham, NC (919) 613-6244	n/a	n/a	n/a	n/a	n/a	n/a	n/a
North Carolina	Clintha Research in High Point, NC (877) 296-1444	Yes	Yes	3.7	Yes	Yes	3.7	4.3
North Dakota	Algorithme in Fargo, ND (701) 356-4000	n/a	n/a	n/a	n/a	n/a	n/a	n/a
North Dakota	Novum in Fargo, ND (877) 586-6886	n/a	n/a	n/a	n/a	n/a	n/a	n/a
Ohio	CTI in Cincinnati, OH (513) 598-9290	n/a	n/a	n/a	n/a	n/a	n/a	n/a
Ohio	Medpace in Cincinnati, OH (800) 730-5779	Yes	Yes	3.5	n/a	Yes	4.1	4
Ohio	Ohio Clinical in Columbus, OH (614) 732-4971	No	Yes	2.2	Yes	Yes	4.7	2.3
Ohio	New Horizons Clinical 9395 Kenwood Rd Unit 101 (513)733-8688	n/a	n/a	n/a	n/a	n/a	n/a	n/a
Pennsylvania	Novum in Pittsburgh, PA (412) 363-3300	n/a	n/a	n/a	n/a	n/a	n/a	n/a
Pennsylvania	Thomas Jefferson at Philadelphia, PA (215) 955-6084	No	Yes	3.5	No	Yes	3.7	2.5
Pennsylvania	U Penn in Philadelphia, PA (215) 662-4484	n/a	n/a	n/a	n/a	n/a	n/a	n/a

State	Facility	Scrubs	Cam phone	Food	Washer /Dryer	Wi-fi	Pay	Rating
Tennessee	NOCCR in Knoxville, TN (865) 305-9100	No	Yes	2.0	Yes	Yes	4.7	3
Texas	PPD in Austin, TX (512) 447-2985	n/a	Yes	2.5	They wash	Yes	4.3	2.2
Texas	WorldWide in San Antonio, TX (210) 635-1500	n/a	n/a	n/a	n/a	n/a	n/a	n/a
Texas	ICON in San Antonio, TX (210) 255-5437	n/a	Yes	4	Yes	Yes	3.5	4.6
Texas	Novum in Houston, TX (800) 586-0365	Yes	Yes	4.3	Yes	Yes	2	2.4
Texas	LabCorp in Dallas, TX (866) 429-3700 *VCT	No	Yes	3	Yes	Yes	3.5	2.3
Texas	NASA in Houston, TX (281) 483-0123	n/a	n/a	n/a	n/a	n/a	n/a	n/a
Utah	PRA* in South Salt Lake, UT (801) 269-8200 *VCT	Yes	Yes	4	No	Yes	4.5	4.5
Wisconsin	LabCorp in Madison, WI (801) 269-8200 *VCT	No	Yes	3.5	They wash	Yes	4.2	3.9
Wisconsin	Spaulding* in West Bend, WI (262) 334-6020	No	Yes	3.3	Yes	n/a	4.4	3.3

**Also there is a clinical trial location in the United Kingdom (England). This location is Covance Clinical Trials which has two locations:

- Leeds, UK
- Liverpool, UK

Their contact number is: 0113 394 5200.

***And lastly there's three locations in Canada, which are:

State	Facility	Scrubs	Cam phone	Food	Washer /Dryer	Wi-fi	Pay	Rating
Canada	Pharma Medica Research Inc. Scarborough, ON (416) 759-5554	n/a	n/a	n/a	n/a	n/a	n/a	3.9
Canada	Syneos Health Montréal Montreal, QC (866) 263-7427	n/a	n/a	n/a	n/a	n/a	n/a	3.8
Canada	Syneos Health Quebec, QC (418) 527-3476	n/a	n/a	n/a	n/a	n/a	n/a	4.4

All of this information is subject to change; facilities open and close all the time. VCT can be added at any time so I suggest calling/Googling any potential company that you might be interested in first before making any plans. Do your due diligence and find all the information you think is necessary for you to participate.

As you can see, some areas of the US are better located than others. I would say the East Coast, mainly the mid- and northern parts (stopping at NJ/NY/CT), the Midwest, and Texas, Missouri, Wisconsin, etc., are the best. Many subjects simply make a few thousand dollars at one facility and then the hit the road and travel to other, more lucrative locations.

One other thing that I would suggest taking into consideration is being aware of the winter months. I wouldn't want to get trapped in a snowstorm and get stranded out there in states such as Wisconsin or Midwest cities like Chicago, St. Louis or Cleveland. This almost happened to me when I did a study in Buffalo, New York. There was an almost two-foot snowstorm, but the natives didn't think much of it because they were used to it. Everything turned out okay.

And again, please beware of VCT, I listed above which facilities participate in this. The standard with mostly all study protocol and clinics is a 30-day washout period. You normally have to wait before you can screen for another study. Some specific studies even require 45, 60, 90 or more days that you have to wait, but 30 is the standard.

If you screened and/or did a study at a clinic that had VCT and you went to another facility the next day that didn't have VCT, they would have no idea that you're screening or did a study somewhere else. But if both clinics have VCT, they would know and you could get in trouble with both of them— anywhere from a verbal warning to getting suspended or banned (rare) after two warnings. So I would be aware of this and take this into serious consideration before doing so. I would also ask a clinic if they have VCT before making a screening (even if not listed above) because this is a fairly new system that a clinic could add at any time.

I mentioned this earlier, but I can't overstate how important this is. Make sure if you decide to screen or check in to another study, that the first study you did or are doing doesn't contain a narcotic drug (vast majority don't) because this will definitely show up in the drug screen test of the next study that you're screening for if it has only been a few days. Something like anesthesia would definitely show up in a drug screen. Yes, most narcotic drugs are out of your system fairly quick (a few days), but just be aware and do your due diligence.

There are many, many more clinical facilities around the US that I did not mention, but the ones above are the locations that are the most lucrative and worth traveling to. Each state has smaller clinics that have studies that you can make anywhere from ten to a few hundred dollars, but I didn't think they were worth mentioning because no one is going to travel from, let's say, Atlanta, Georgia, to Pittsburgh, Pennsylvania for $200. But in the near future, I will come out with Part II of *Prospering in a Pandemic*, adding these locations for the local people and the working people who don't want to or don't have the time to travel that far.

Also, many of these other locations have clinical trials for people with pre-existing ailments. For example, to qualify you might need to have a history of cancer, high blood pressure, high cholesterol, diabetes, obesity, fungus, acne, missing teeth, HIV, AIDS or some even have studies for children. But like I previously mentioned, I will put all of those into Part II along with some other important tips and tricks.

New facilities open and close all the time. So the more networking you do, the more you will find out about other spots that have either opened, reopened under another name, or closed indefinitely. Like I previously mentioned, there are hundreds of smaller locations that I have not listed because it would be way too many. I only concentrated on the higher-paying ones that are currently out there.

ABOUT THE AUTHOR

I got introduced to clinical trials starting out as a medical technician for a clinic. This facility I will not name is still in business, but they are not conducting clinical trials themselves. They're a big pharmaceutical company and now outsource all of their clinical testing to other facilities that perform this part of the operation for them.

While working there, my duties were mainly blood processing but not limited to just this. I would also perform vital signs, temperature, EKG's etc. The funny thing about this is I never did formal schooling for any of this. They took a chance on me, giving me on-the-job training and everything turned out great. This is the reason I couldn't just go to another clinic that did clinical trials. I was never certified through the state. I would only be able to go to a company that was willing to re-train or sponsor me the same way my original company did.

Throughout those years, I've been a part of a medical team that has overseen plenty of studies and seen many subjects make a lot of money. So when the doors closed at this particular company and my unemployment money ran out, it occurred to me that I could do a medical study myself. I basically knew everything about them and how to get started, and that's exactly what I did.

I did a few studies immediately after and made a decent amount of money, and even more after that. Two years passed and I had made enough to be financially stable, but I always felt that there was more to this, like I was leaving money on the table somewhere. I felt like I knew way more about this than the average subject. Even though I felt like I had made decent money at that point (around $90,000), I still was eager to profit even more from my knowledge that I had of medical research. I should have purchased several houses or opened a business by now. But I hadn't at that point. All I had was some cash, nice cars, clothes, and vacations.

Then a light bulb popped into my head! I could write a book on clinical trials. There are so many people that don't know about studies, but wished they did! For the price of your average dinner, I could give people the opportunity to make tens of thousands of dollars. There's no other (legal) good fortune like this in the world that I know of that involves no skill, luck or upfront money. And I can't over emphasize that it's not a get-rich-quick scheme. If you're in decent health, you're gonna make some money quickly. *It's that simple.* And even more, your investment in this is so little that it's basically a no-brainer, so why not give it a shot?

So, in order for me to successfully and accurately provide my audience with this information, I had to make my rounds to most of the facilities to rate them, experience them, and know firsthand what to expect when you visit each location. I haven't been to all of them, but I've been to enough of them, and know plenty of other subects who have also, to give you a good idea of what to expect at most of these locations.

I can't emphasize enough how much time studies free up for you to do so many things that a 9-5 just doesn't provide. I procrastinated on writing the book for a while, then finally I did a 24-day study some years back, and I used every minute of my free time to put together this masterpiece. I still sat on my almost-finished product for years, never releasing it until now, which I believe is the perfect time to do so. Considering Covid and the loss of jobs and income that will only get worse, this is the quintessential time to release this manual.

I'm a good-hearted person, and it would eat me up inside if I sold someone something that wasn't as advertised. If I ever ripped someone off even a few dollars, I would think about it for months. But in the case of *Prospering In A Pandemic,* I'm sure most will be satisfied customers, especially after completing just one study.

I am absolutely positive that this book will save plenty of lives financially and become a life jacket for thousands who had no idea where their next dollar was going to come from. I hope everyone who makes a purchase also makes a profit and put themselves and their families in a much better position to take care of bills that they probably thought would never have gotten satisfied otherwise. 🙏

CONCLUSION

I know this was a lot of information to grasp and absorb but it's really not as difficult as it sounds. Most people did their first study without even using a tenth of the information I provided you. And I have come to the conclusion that you will either love the study game or you will hate it. The funny part about those who are not too fond of doing studies is that many will still participate periodically because the money is so good. I suggest, depending on your geographical location, just calling up the closest clinic to you and finding out what they have available and set up a screening. Try that one out, complete it, and then you will have enough money to travel and try out a better, more lucrative study. Then the process repeats itself, and soon you will find yourself in a much better financial positon. Also, a huge tip I would suggest when traveling is, search for a Airbnb or hostel that's in the area of the clinical facility you're visiting instead of a hotel, this will drastically decrease your traveling expenses.

Like I mentioned in a previous chapter, try to always arrive first and pick the earliest screening date available. I don't care if it's checking in, screening, doing a physical or doing a second screening on another day; always try to be one of the first. You don't want to lose your spot to someone else just because that particular location was choosing subjects on a first-come, first-served basis.

One other huge thing that I haven't mentioned yet is taxes. Taxes are not taken out of your checks, and if you make over $600, you will have to pay taxes on income earned. At each screening, you will fill out a W-9 and at the end of the year, you will receive a 1099 in the mail similar to a W-2. My suggestion would be to save every receipt that you ever get, from food, to bus, train, phone bill, tolls, gas, etc. You will be amazed at how much this will accumulate to in write-offs. This will work wonders for you when it's time to do your taxes. And if you have children to claim, you will definitely be getting back a nice refund.

In a nutshell, medical studies have been nothing short of being heaven-sent for a lot of people. So many folks would have been in terrible financial predicaments if it wasn't for the existence of studies. And it's not just the subjects themselves, it's also their families, their loved ones, relatives, etc., that they have taken care of because of this opportunity. Tens of millions of dollars in bills, vacations, business ventures, clothes, shelter, etc., have been paid for with study proceeds.

I will close by saying I know this book is going to help a lot of people financially. Studies have provided me with plenty of money and time to do things that many only dream of, along with a boatload of knowledge on health and the human body.

Are there side effects? Of course this is possible! But that goes with almost everything our bodies consume, from the food we eat to the air we breathe. In general, I can honestly say that medical studies are primarily safe for the most part.

And like I always say, I would rather get paid to take a pill than pay that same pharmaceutical company hundred of dollars to take that same exact pill. And probably have the same or worse results because most people with a prescription are taking their medication on a daily and consistent basis, not just once or a few times like you would do in an average medical study.

Again, another very helpful treat to my study family is keep your eyes open for the Patreon and Only Fans page under the name Blood_Money. An also as a bonus we're adding a subscription-based format that will provide you with important tools for tricks of this trade along with up to the minute news of the newest & latest studies that just posted. This will definitely be extremely beneficial to anyone who's interested in being successful in the medical study world or just curious and would like to know more pertaining to this relatively unknown line of employment. This will give you a greater advantage with signing up and screening first which is a huge plus! Also I will be providing little tips to aid you on having a healthier and smoother study career. And of course there's also Instagram, Facebook, and YouTube. The domain name will be "Prospering In A Pandemic (Make Wealth with Your Health)" on all platforms.

Lastly I would like to give a huge shout out to BioTech, Novavax, Pfizer, GlaxoSmithKline, AstraZeneca, Moderna, J & J, Merck, and Sanofi amongst others for their recent pledge to listen to the science in the quest for the future developments of Covid-19 cures and preventions.

Remember, stay hydrated my friends, stay hydrated!

Good luck to all . . .

The End!

www.ingramcontent.com/pod-product-compliance
Lightning Source LLC
LaVergne TN
LVHW011730060526
838200LV00051B/3112